Nelson Multi-Media Group
Presents

Jesus Among Other Gods

By Ravi Zacharias

An EZ Lesson Video Curriculum

Leader's Guide

with Jonathan Ziman
and Neil Wilson of Livingstone

D0110836

Jesus Among Other Gods

Published by Nelson Multi-Media Group
A division of Thomas Nelson Publishers
P.O. Box 141000, Nashville, TN 37214

Produced with the assistance of the Livingstone Corporation. Contributors: Jonathan Ziman, Ashley Taylor, Neil Wilson.

ISBN 0-8499-8845-4

Table of Contents

A Note from Ravi 5

Attention Group Leader 7

The Effective Teacher 9

Tips for Leading an Effective Discussion 11

Brief Summary of Belief Systems Discussed
in *Jesus Among Other Gods* 15

Introduction to the Student's Guide 17

Lesson 1
The Anatomy of Faith and the Quest for Reason 19

Lesson 2
A Taste for the Soul 31

Lesson 3
Is God the Source of My Suffering? 43

Lesson 4
Is There a Gardener? 61

About Ravi Zacharias 79

A Note from Ravi

I would like to welcome you to this four-part study of *Jesus Among Other Gods*. My hope, of course, is that you have already read the book, and if you haven't, that you will make that a priority because I think you will be able to track the ideas in the study much more rigorously with that material already engaged in your thinking.

I sincerely desire that this study not only be informative to you and inspirational for you, but I hope and pray that it will also be life transforming. I will be honest with you; it was that very way in my own life.

You see, the challenge of writing this book and filming these presentations was very real. We are living in a day where sensitivities are high, where tolerance and pluralism are buzzwords, and there's a lot of important reality we must bear in mind when we are dealing with that kind of a challenge. However, let us be absolutely clear that when we present the nature of truth, as you will soon see, exclusivity is implicit in that claim. You can sense this in the subtitle of the book, The Absolute Claims of the Christian Message. That, in a phrase, is the challenge we face, to speak about the absolute claims of Christ in a world that increasingly accepts the idea that the only absolute is that there are no absolutes!

How do we approach a subject like this, though? I remember two proverbs that I was raised with growing up in India. One of them was this: When you're touching your nose, you can either touch it directly, or you can go the long way around. You are certainly welcome to try this at home. The proverb simply points out that you can't cut straight into some tough material. Sometimes you have to go the long way in the challenge of ideas.

The other proverb was one my mother taught me when she repeatedly told me, "After you've cut off a person's nose, there's no point in giving them a rose to smell." If we cut an idea down or a person off at his or her knees, and then offer them the sweet savor of Christ, we probably shouldn't expect to get a positive response.

As we examine in this study the questions that Jesus answered for those who were attracted to Him and those who attacked Him, we will be thinking about the nature of the truth as well as the way the truth can be presented. The way Jesus answered questions demonstrates that no other claimant to divine or prophetic status would have ever answered those questions the same way. Jesus revealed a marvelous uniqueness that I pray you will not miss. I know this—spending time with Jesus will transform your life.

Thank you for joining me in this study of *Jesus Among Other Gods*.

Attention Group Leader

THIS BOOK IS FOR YOU. It may look just like the one that everyone in the group is using, but it's different. Here's how:

Leader Notes

The outside column of every lesson page is entitled "Leader Notes." In the regular lesson book, the column is entitled, "Lesson Notes," and is blank, providing a place for the user to write personal comments and notes on every page.

In your column, however, you will find the following items, designed to help you lead your group.

1. Objective. At the start of every lesson, you will find the objective for that lesson. Because each lesson has been written to give users a rational and an emotive experience, the objective will state that as a result of this lesson participants will learn or understand a theological truth (usually stated "understand) and appreciate what God has done for them (or feel deeply, and so forth). The objective drives the lesson and keeps it on track.

2. Time Notes. At each section of a lesson, you will find a suggested amount of time that specific part of the lesson should take. These are approximations, but they have been provided to keep each lesson within 60 minutes.

3. Suggestions & Tips. Throughout each lesson, you will find directions for which questions to ask, alternate activities to use, and other tips for teaching the specific lesson. Some of the questions in the lesson will work better in a group than in personal study and vice versa. And because group dynamics always plays a part in how well a group discusses and learns together, reminders and special tips have been included to enhance the group experience and keep the group on track.

Red-Letter Helps

Your copy also includes suggested answers for the factual questions in the lessons. This will hopefully assist you in guiding the discussion. In your preparation, however, try to think about your own answers before simply relying on what is supplied. You may have some helpful insights to offer!

Special Articles

Immediately following this introductory material, you will find three articles that will help you in your role as group leader.

The first, "The Effective Teacher," by David Veerman, provides a valuable checklist to help you make sure you are ready to teach.

The second article, "Tips for Leading an Effective Discussion," is filled with practical suggestions for getting people talking and helping them discover biblical truths.

The third article, "Brief Summary of the Belief Systems Discussed in *Jesus Among Other Gods*," can also be found in the student's guide and is designed to answer basic questions about those religions.

The four individual lessons each have the following divisions:

Review—This begins each lesson except for Lesson 1 and briefly summarizes the content of the previous lessons. Group members may arrive with questions from last week. Keep this light and keep it moving.

Warm-Up—The purpose of this section is to help group members begin thinking about the main topic of the lesson.

The Video—Introduces the theme of the session's video segment. Be sure to have the VCR and TV turned on and the tape cued to the beginning of the correct video segment. Encourage the group to use the sections in their workbooks set up for notes on the video.

Reviewing the Lesson—This section allows the group to discuss the video itself and clarify the points made by Ravi in his presentation.

Bible Focus—This section of the lesson focuses on several key Bible passages used by Ravi in his presentation. This should be the longest and most intense part of each of the sessions, allowing God's Word to speak to the issues and questions.

Taking It Home—At the end of each lesson, this section contains personal application questions and suggestions on implementing the lessons in day-to-day living.

Each lesson also includes a number of quotes from Ravi's book, other authors, and verbatim video clips. These are meant to be supplemental and some of the questions refer to those sidebars.

About the video segments—four are included on the tape, one for each lesson. The segment for Lesson 1 includes a brief welcome and introduction by Ravi.

The rest of this book is the same. In other words, everything in the student book is included in this volume. To prepare for the lesson, be sure to answer all the questions yourself, beforehand.

The Effective Teacher

To be an effective teacher, you need to remember the following:

KNOW YOUR LORD. This may seem obvious, but too often Sunday school teachers and small group leaders approach their groups totally in their own strength. That is, they count on a combination of their skill and cleverness and the material to make each session work. Instead, we need to teach in the power of the Holy Spirit. This means that your relationship with God must be current and close. And it certainly means praying about the class or group meeting, each lesson, and each group member.

KNOW YOUR MATERIAL. The caricature of the typical Sunday school teacher has him or her staying up late the night before to read the lesson or driving to church with the lesson on his or her lap, "preparing" for the lesson on the fly. That's the wrong way. Instead, teachers should read and work through the lesson early in the week, to become familiar with the content and to see if any special preparations are necessary and supplemental materials would be helpful. If you prepare in advance, during the week, you can think about the upcoming lesson and how to add creativity, depth, and special adaptations to your group. The night before, then, you can *review* the lesson.

KNOW YOURSELF. Few things are more embarrassing than watching someone trying awkwardly to be someone else: the speaker trying to imitate a television evangelist, the singer giving her solo a show-biz flair, the un-funny guy trying to be a comedian. God has given you a unique gift-mix, and He wants you to use your gifts to serve Him and build up His church. If you know that you are weak in a certain area, enlist the help of those who possess the gifts that can complement yours. You also have a unique teaching style. Again, use it and beware of your tendencies. For example, if you know that you tend to get off on tangents and ramble, tell your spouse or a close friend to signal you when that begins to occur.

KNOW YOUR GROUP. A good teacher can teach almost anyone, even a room full of suspicious strangers. But it's much easier to get through to people with whom you have a relationship. Although group membership may change from week to week, you probably will have a core of regular attendees. So after your first week together, you should work hard at learning names and something about each person. If you are team-teaching this class or your spouse is with you, that other person can fill you in on details about people in the group whom you don't know very well. The more you know about a group, the better you can tailor each lesson, understand what's behind questions and comments, make the group enjoyable and personal, and draw the group close.

KNOW YOUR ENVIRONMENT AND EQUIPMENT. What is the design of the room? How will the chairs be arranged? What about the lighting and acoustics? What special equipment will you need? Where will you stand? What about the room temperature? You should have the answers to these questions well before your first class. If you have been assigned a small room that holds thirty comfortably but fifty have signed up for the class, you probably will have to change rooms or your teaching approach (for example, no breaking into small groups). If you need a VCR and TV for a lesson, make sure you have them and know how to operate them (and get to the room early to cue the tape). As the Boy Scouts say, "Be prepared."

Jim Rayburn, the founder of Young Life, said, "It's a sin to bore a kid with the Gospel." Taking that a step further, it's surely sinful to bore anyone with God, His Word, or His Son. God wants us to be effective teachers as we share His truth with others.

Dave Veerman

Tips for Leading an Effective Discussion

Groups do not live by lecture alone. Regardless of the type of group, any good discussion will involve asking and answering questions. Although anyone should be allowed to ask questions, it is your responsibility, as a leader, to have good questions to get the discussion started and then keep it going. This means that you should *prepare* for each group meeting or class. Don't just show up and depend on the group dynamics and your sparkling personality to carry the day. If there is content to be conveyed, help to be offered, Scripture to be studied, and so forth, you must be prepared.

Preparation begins by thinking through the topic at hand and studying thoroughly any material you have that the group is using. Preparation also means thinking through the questions you will be asking. Even if you are using questions that someone else has written, look them over and adapt them to your group.

Here are some general guidelines for creating and adapting questions:

Ask questions that provoke thought. Avoid questions that can be answered by yes or no or another one-word response. That will kill a discussion faster than you can say, "Anyone else?"

Galatians 6:1 says, "Brethren, if a man is overtaken in any trespass, you who are spiritual restore such a one in a spirit of gentleness, considering yourself lest you also be tempted"

In discussing this passage, some leaders might ask:
• Should Christians help other Christians?
• Have you ever done anything wrong?
It may seem obvious that those are poor questions to ask, but Sunday school classes and small groups everywhere are filled with them.

Better questions would include:
• What could Paul have in mind by the phrase 'overtaken in any trespass'?
• What can a Christian do to help another Christian back onto the right path?
• What are some examples of someone exercising a 'spirit of gentleness'?

Almost all yes or no questions already have a correct answer for which the questioner is looking. So instead of asking the obvious, assume the answer and ask a "what," "why," or a "how" question—force the group to think. Instead of asking, "Should children obey their parents?" ask, "Why do you think God tells children to obey their parents?" or "When is it difficult for a child to obey his or her parents?"

Ask questions that are simple and easy to understand. If a person has to ask for the questions to be repeated, the question is probably too complicated.

If you are discussing loneliness, you might want to ask about the reasons for loneliness. Here's an example of a question that is complex and difficult to understand: "Why, and according to many studies it's true, do you think kids are lonely today, as opposed to my generation when it seemed to be a more carefree era?" The question is complicated because it contains extraneous and confusing phrases. A simple, direct question would be: "Why do you think kids today are lonely?"

Ask interesting questions. As you consider each question, put yourself in the shoes of a person in the group. Would *you* be interested in answering that question? The best questions almost beg to be discussed.

Sometimes the topic itself is boring because it's not controversial or a felt need. "Pollution," for example, would be a boring topic for anyone to discuss because no one is *for* it.

Even very important topics can be boring because people aren't *feeling* them right now. "Death" is a good example of such a topic. Most people, especially young people, don't think much about dying, and they live as though they are immortal. Although death is a vital subject to consider and discuss, it may be difficult to get much interaction. But think of how the group would probably talk if someone they know had just died.

With topics that aren't currently relevant or naturally interesting, you will have to work even harder at your questions, perhaps using case studies or real-life situations (for example, from your life or the news) to set up a moral dilemma, build tension, or create a conflict to be resolved.

Know where you will begin. Your first question is most important because it will set the tone for the rest of the discussion and because you will usually get to ask that one. This first question, therefore, should be nonthreatening and light, almost like an icebreaker, helping everyone begin to talk and think about the topic. How you react to the answers to this first question is also very important. Be positive and grateful, not disagreeing or correcting.

A good opener for a discussion about the family might be to have everyone describe their favorite family vacation or their favorite television sitcom. One way to begin talking about fear would be to discuss scary movies that they have seen. An opening question for a discussion of the sovereignty of God could be: "What are some of the more disturbing news stories you've seen on the news or read about lately?"

Next, be ready with a follow-up question or two to get into the topic. In the discussion about the sovereignty of God, for example, you could follow with: "Where is God in all of this bad news? Why doesn't He do something about the problems in the world?"

Keep it going. The best way to keep the discussion going, with energy and direction, is to remember your role as listener and learner. As the discussion leader (facilitator), you will be asking questions and encouraging group members to respond and interact. At times, you will also have to act as referee, making sure that one person speaks at a time and reminding everyone of the ground rules.

But for the discussion to flourish, remember and heed the following "dos and don'ts."

1. *Don't interrupt* (unless a person is going way off on a tangent). Remember, you are a listener too. So let each person say what is honestly on his or her heart and mind, even if it's wrong or the opposite of what you think.
2. *Don't judge.* If you are asking good questions, then often there will not be right or wrong answers. So don't jump on someone who says something off the wall or heretical—let him or her speak. Of course we believe that there is ultimate truth to be discovered and shared. But let the group discover the truth together; don't dish it out to them.
3. *Don't make speeches or preach.* Even if you know more than the rest of the group put together, your words of wisdom probably will kill discussion and fall on deaf ears. If someone asks for your expert advice or your opinion on something, give it calmly, slowly, and concisely. Don't give the impression that you have all the answers and that your way is the only way.
4. *Do probe and ask for clarification.* If someone makes a statement, feel free to ask what he or she meant if you didn't understand or you think it may have been unclear to others. Or you could repeat the person's point in other words: for example, "I hear you saying that you agree with Ted because . . . . Is that right?"
5. *Do affirm and encourage.* Look for opportunities to compliment individuals for their participation: for example, "That was a good insight, Mary. Thanks for sharing it." "That's good. I've never thought of that before." "Yeah, yeah, I can see that—thanks." This will let everyone know that they can make a valuable contribution to the discussion.
6. *Do try to get everyone involved.* If someone is monopolizing the discussion, you could say something like, "Tanya, you've contributed a lot of great thoughts tonight, but there may be some others who haven't spoken up yet who have something to say. Let's give them a chance to speak, and then I'll come back to you, OK?"

If certain members are quiet, it probably won't help to single them out by asking them to comment on an issue. Instead, watch for a spark of interest and then fan it. Someone might nod in agreement with something that was said, and you could say: "You look like you agree with that, Len. Do you want to add anything?" And if they do say something, be quick to thank them for their participation. If certain people never say much, let them know it's all right by catching their eye and giving a quick wink or smile. You may want to talk with them afterward and explain that whenever they're ready to talk in the group, everyone will be ready to listen.

Dave Veerman

Brief Summary of Belief Systems Discussed in *Jesus Among Other Gods:* Hinduism, Buddhism, Islam

Hinduism

Hinduism is a varied system of religion, philosophy, and cultural practices born in India. Hindus share a core belief in reincarnation and a supreme being of many forms and natures.

Hinduism dates to 1500 B.C. as a system of ritual and multiple gods (polytheism). Shiva, Vishnu, Kali or Ganesh are among the most popular deities, but countless millions of additional minor gods tied to a particular village or family are also worshiped. Hinduism is a very complex system where popular practice and philosophical theory do not always meet. Systemizing it is almost impossible.

Hinduism holds that opposing religious theories are aspects of one eternal truth.

The goal of Hinduism is to achieve Moksha or Nirvana, a release from rebirths and a merging with the Oneness of the universe.

Hinduism holds that human life is a cycle of reincarnation. Rebirth can be in human or animal form. To Hindus, the circumstances of the new birth are determined by the good and evil of past actions—the Law of Karma.

The self is ultimately divinized in Hinduism.

The focus is more on a way of life than on a doctrine of belief. That is why it is sometimes hard to differentiate between religion and culture.

The earliest and primary Hindu scriptures are known as the "Vedas." There are other writings placed in various categories of authority.

The vast majority of the world's 750 million Hindus live in India.

Buddhism

Buddhism is a religion of great variation, yet its central teachings are that suffering is an inherent part of life and that liberation from suffering comes from moral and mental self-purification.

Buddhism grew out of the teachings of Siddhartha Gautama (563–483 B.C.), who later became known as Buddha, "the enlightened one."

Buddha left Hinduism because he could not accept the final authority of the Vedas or subscribe to the caste system.

Buddha is revered not as God but as a spiritual master who points the way to enlightenment.

At the core of Buddha's teaching are four basic or "noble" truths:
1. life is suffering,
2. the cause of suffering is desire,
3. suffering can be ended by getting rid of desire, and
4. freedom from desire is achieved via an eightfold path of right views, right intention, right speech, right action, right livelihood, right effort, right-mindedness, and right contemplation.

The goal of Buddhism is to be freed from the cycle of death and rebirth.

A Buddhist who ceases to desire is "Enlightened" and achieves the state of Nirvana, an abstract nothingness.

There is no real self in Buddhism.

Buddhism, strongest in eastern and central Asia, has some three hundred million adherents.

Buddhism is uncertain about the existence of a personal God.

Islam

Islam teaches that there is one God, Allah. It focuses on submission to God and acceptance of Mohammed as the chief and last prophet of God.

Islam was founded in Arabia by Mohammed (c. A.D. 570–632). A person who practices Islam is known as a Muslim.

Islam takes its name from the Arabic word for "devout submission to the will of God."

Muslims accept their scriptures, the Koran, as the speech of God to Mohammed, and they believe that God Himself is the author.

Muslims observe the five "pillars" of Islam:
1. the declaration of faith,
2. prayer,
3. fasting,
4. giving alms, and
5. a pilgrimage to Mecca.

Islam has more than one billion adherents from Africa to the Middle East and parts of Asia and Europe.

Many predominantly Muslim nations have closed their borders to Christian missionaries or made evangelism illegal.

Islam sees Jesus as one of the major prophets, but to call Jesus God's Son is blasphemous.

It accepts as genuine some of the miracles of Jesus, including the virgin birth, and even His power to raise the dead.

NOTE: The above information was downloaded from the official site connected with this study and Ravi's book:
http://www.jesusamongothergods.com/world.htm

Introduction to the Student's Guide

Welcome to the student workbook for *Jesus Among Other Gods*. We hope that this will be a valuable experience for you as you make your way through the pages of this book. These four lessons have been written to encourage, inspire, and challenge you as you journey through a world increasingly crowded by the competing claims of gods and religions that do not acknowledge Jesus Christ as Lord.

This interactive study incorporates material from the book *Jesus Among Other Gods* by Ravi Zacharias, and has been designed to accompany personal and group study of the four-part video presentation featuring Ravi Zacharias. While the book itself is not required for an effective study, a wealth of helpful and more detailed material can be found in the book that will enrich any believer's awareness of the belief systems that challenge Christianity today.

You can either use this workbook as part of a group study or on your own—both methods will help you grow significantly. To accompany this workbook, a leader's guide has been provided for leaders of a small group study. Leaders wishing to make use of this material are encouraged to provide a workbook for each student, as copying all or part of the workbooks is legally prohibited.

You will notice that each lesson is divided into separate sections: Warm-up, The Video, Reviewing the Lesson, Bible Focus, and Taking It Home.

Warm-up helps you to begin thinking about the topic of the lesson from your own experience.
The Video introduces the video lesson and provides note space for Ravi's presentation.
Reviewing the Lesson leads a person or group through the content in the video, allowing the viewers to clarify and internalize Ravi's presentation.
Bible Focus examines each of the Bible passages used by Ravi in developing the theme of the session. The studies focus on both an understanding and application of the Scripture passages.
Taking It Home assists participants in considering how the teaching of the session impacts their own lives.

In the video package, four video segments feature Ravi Zacharias, filmed in international locations, sharing his experiences and insights as a widely traveled apologist for the Christian faith.

Further Resources

Consult the website www.jesusamongothergods.com for other resources and help in sharing Christ with those around you.

Lesson 1

"The Anatomy of Faith and the Quest for Reason"

Warm-up

Before watching the first video segment, read the following quote about today's attitudes from Ravi Zacharias's book, *Jesus Among Other Gods:*

> Philosophically, you can believe anything, so long as you do not claim it to be true. Morally, you can practice anything, so long as you do not claim that it is a "better" way. Religiously, you can hold to anything, so long as you do not bring Jesus Christ into it. If a spiritual idea is eastern, it is granted critical immunity; if western, it is thoroughly criticized. Thus, a journalist can walk into a church and mock its carryings on, but he or she dare not do the same if the ceremony is from the eastern fold. Such is the mood at the end of the twentieth century (p. vii).

To what degree do you think Ravi's comments are accurate? List some personal experiences that may support (or perhaps refute) his claim that people will let you "believe anything, so long as you do not claim it to be true."

_____

_____

_____

Ravi goes on to ask "How does one in a mood such as this communicate the message of Jesus Christ, in which truth and absoluteness are not only assumed, but also sustained?" What responses have you received when you have tried to share the message of Jesus Christ, given this "mood" we seem to be experiencing today?

Many people today feel justified in attacking Christianity because it is not "tolerant" enough.

_____

_____

_____

Unless this is already a small group study, consider discussing these questions in groups of three or four.
Up to 5 minutes

Challenge the group to think about "absolutes" and how claiming an absolute will always make some people feel that they are being accused of being "wrong." Today's society does not want to be "wrong." There is even an attitude that tries to convince people that "sins" and "mistakes" were actually "wonderful" at the time. You may hear a lot of people today saying, "I have no regrets." It's a philosophy that denies that they did anything bad, or that they should feel guilty about it.

Emphasize that in many ways tolerance = ambivalence, intellectual laziness, and ignorance. "Love your neighbor" is what we are called to do. Not "tolerate lies and deception."

Leader Notes

When Jesus quoted Deuteronomy 6:5, He purposely included the mind as one of the personal channels of our love for God (Mark 12:28–30). By doing so, He clarified the scope of our relationship with God. We are expected to love the Lord completely. In this case, our love must be conscious and thoughtful.

In a world where faith is often described as a characteristic of people who don't think, Jesus' words point to the importance of engaging our minds as a central aspect of what we believe. Jesus spoke of Himself as the truth (John 14:6). The Bible repeatedly claims to be true and reliable (Psalm 19:7–11; 119:151; 2 Timothy 3:16). Truth keeps the mind healthy.

Every day your mind has to digest large quantities of mental junk food. If you do not include truth in your thought diet, you will have a malnourished mind. The daily discipline of thinking about God's Word will result in spiritual health.

Neil Wilson

20 Minutes

Make sure you have previewed the video so that you can concentrate on your group's reactions to Ravi's presentation. Read over for the group the four points Ravi will cover so they will know what to expect. Encourage the group to make notes they can use during the discussion that will follow.
Video length: approximately 17 minutes

The Video

Perhaps one of the most frequent questions we encounter from nonbelievers is, "Where is the proof for what you believe?" Two thousand years ago the Pharisees posed a similar question to Jesus, asking, "What sign do You show to us, since You do these things?" (John 2:18). In the first video segment, entitled "The Anatomy of Faith and the Quest for Reason," Ravi will address these questions within the framework of four principal postulates. Use the space below to jot down some notes on each point as Ravi walks us through this first lesson.

1. The absolute nature of truth.

_____

_____

_____

2. The tension between faith and reason.

_____

_____

_____

3. What Jesus said about the sign or evidence.

_____

_____

_____

4. The uniqueness of His message.

_____

_____

_____

Other video notes you want to remember:

_____

_____

_____

Reviewing the Lesson
Ravi opens the video session with a lighthearted poke at those who claim that "all truth is relative." Such a claim is a logical contradiction, since, in an effort to deny the presence of absolutes, the person is making an absolute claim.

> The idea of relativism basically implies that all truth is individually constructed, individually determined, and all values are only individually chosen and subjectively appropriated.
>
> Ravi Zacharias

List some specific situations in which you have encountered relativism recently—perhaps at work, among friends, or on television or in the news.
Examples: "It's okay to commit adultery if you're in love." "It's okay to cheat on your taxes in order to support your family financially." "I believe that I'm a good person, and God will understand that."

_____

_____

_____

How have you responded to relativism in the past? Do you get any new ideas from the video or the book for how you might tackle this in the future?

_____

_____

_____

Discussing the tension between faith and reason, Ravi recounts a time when Bertrand Russell (a famous philosopher) was asked what he would say if, upon his death, God were to ask him to justify his atheism? Bertrand Russell replied, "I will tell Him that He did not give me enough evidence."

Leader Notes

This question and the next may run together in your discussions. The bottom line is that God is under no obligation to prove Himself to us. He is God. He created us. However, He didn't just make us and then leave. He wants a relationship with us, and has given plenty of "evidence" to support a rational belief in Him. The question usually comes down to whether or not someone *wants* to believe.

Try to help them challenge this attitude and question by suggesting they can use some of the following questions:
Why do you need evidence?
If you don't know exactly how much evidence it will take, how does your situation differ from someone who is simply excusing unbelief?
What is so scary about believing in a loving creator who watches over you?
How does demanding evidence from God indicate your assumption about who is really in control of the situation? Often you can witness to people just by being present in their life, so they can see how you respond to life's difficulties. And keep praying for them!

What comes to mind when you think of "evidence for God's existence"? Do you feel that God has given people enough evidence for belief in Him? Why? Why not?

In what ways, if any, is God obliged to prove Himself to us? Read Job 38:1–41:33 for a perspective on this question.
As the created beings, we have no ground to stand upon when it comes to questioning God.

What would constitute "enough" evidence for someone like Bertrand Russell?
Probably nothing. There were many people who saw the miracles of Jesus and still refused to believe. People like Mr. Russell have already made the decision not to believe. Nothing is going to change that except lots of prayer for them and the work of the Holy Spirit.

What approach would you take in order to share the gospel message with someone who feels that "God hasn't given me enough evidence"?

Ravi refers to Dr. Wickramasinghe, a practicing Buddhist who is also a professor of mathematics at the University of Cardiff in Wales, who claims that the chances of randomly obtaining all 2,000 enzymes in the human body is one out of $10^{40,000}$. Ravi's book is even more specific, in pointing out that, ". . . the statistical probability of forming even a single enzyme, the building block of the gene, which is in turn the building block of the cell, is 1 in $10^{40,000}$" (*Jesus Among Other Gods*, p. 65).

Given these numbers, what would be the most "reasonable" response to the belief that we came into existence by random chance?
Statistically it makes more sense that there was a creator.

All too frequently conversations about our origins become arguments about Creationism vs. Darwinism. How could you use these numbers by Dr. Wickramasinghe to move the debate in a different direction?
Get people to focus on the miracle of creation instead of debating evolution. Keep going "back" in time with probing questions:
Where did we come from?
Where did earth come from?
What about the big bang?
What was before that?

How can you counteract the stereotypes that Christians live solely on faith, while the "enlightened" live solely by reason?
Look at the intricacy of the human body, at a flower in a field, or the differences between snowflakes. It is "unreasonable" to think that these all developed over time, on their own, by accident, so to speak. Christians live by both faith and reason. God said He would "confound the wisdom of the wise" (see 1 Corinthians 1:18–20).
Jonathan Ziman

Bible Focus
Read Matthew 12:38–42.

Then some of the scribes and Pharisees answered, saying, "Teacher, we want to see a sign from You."
But He answered and said to them, "An evil and adulterous generation seeks after a sign, and no sign will be given to it except the sign of the prophet Jonah. For as Jonah was three days and three nights in the belly of the great fish, so will the Son of Man be three days and three nights in the heart of the earth. The men of Nineveh will rise in the judgment with this generation and condemn it, because they repented at the preaching of Jonah; and indeed a greater than Jonah is here. The queen of the South will rise up in the judgment with this generation and condemn it, for she came from the ends of the earth to hear the wisdom of Solomon; and indeed a greater than Solomon is here.

Why did the Pharisees and scribes ask to see a sign?
They actually didn't want any proof but were looking for ways to trap Him. Like Bertrand Russell, no amount of evidence would have been enough for them to believe.

_____

_____

Why did Jesus say He refused to give them one?
He knew that a sign would not be enough to convince them.

_____

_____

What is "the sign of the prophet Jonah" to which Jesus referred?
Jesus' death, burial, and resurrection, which are similar to Jonah being swallowed by the whale, held in its belly for three days, and then spit out.

_____

_____

_____

What did Jesus mean when He said the men of Nineveh will condemn "this generation"?
The people of Nineveh were stubborn and sinful. However, when they recognized the voice of God speaking through the prophet Jonah, they repented. By the time of Jesus, however, mankind had become so stubborn that even when God Himself spoke (Jesus), most people refused to repent. And today we encounter the same problem still.

_____

_____

_____

Have you ever asked God for a sign? Why? Why not?

Leader Notes

Remind the group that signs are so easily misinterpreted. The Bible, on the other hand, says that we should put our trust in Jesus, not signs and wonders.

_____

_____

_____

> Jesus is charging that the very motivation that impelled them to demand a sign revealed not only that they were not genuinely seeking the truth, but their resistance to truth, though they were religious, made the hardened pagan look better than they. In other words, it was not the absence of a sign that troubled them. It was the *message* behind the signs that provoked their discomfort. If Jesus could sustain who He was, the ramifications for them were cataclysmic. Everything they pursued and owned, every vestige of inordinate power they enjoyed, was dependent on their being the determiners of other people's destinies. Sometimes religion can be the greatest roadblock to true spirituality.
>
> (*Jesus Among Other Gods*, p. 56)

Read Hebrews 11:1.
Now faith is the substance of things hoped for, the evidence of things not seen.

Skim through all of Hebrews 11. What an amazing list of great acts of faith! Which acts of faith listed in Hebrews 11 stand out most to you? Why?

_____

_____

_____

List some ways that you have acted on faith this week.

_____

_____

_____

What motivates you to act on faith?
A realization that I can't do anything without God. The alternative is doubt, worry, too much reliance on the self, etc. The Holy Spirit guides us and prompts us to be more faithful.

_____

_____

_____

In what areas of your life has this study encouraged you to walk by faith this week—in your job, at home, among friends?

> Faith in the biblical sense is substantive, based on the knowledge that the One in whom that faith is placed has proven that He is worthy of that trust. In its essence, *faith is a confidence in the person of Jesus Christ and in His power, so that even when His power does not serve my end, my confidence in Him remains because of who He is.* Faith for the Christian is the response of trust based on who Jesus Christ claimed to be, and it results in a life that brings both mind and heart in a commitment of love to Him.
>
> (*Jesus Among Other Gods*, p. 58)

Read John 2:13–22.

Now the Passover of the Jews was at hand, and Jesus went up to Jerusalem. And He found in the temple those who sold oxen and sheep and doves, and the moneychangers doing business. When He had made a whip of cords, He drove them all out of the temple, with the sheep and the oxen, and poured out the changers' money and overturned the tables. And He said to those who sold doves, "Take these things away! Do not make My Father's house a house of merchandise!"

Then His disciples remembered that it was written, "Zeal for Your house has eaten Me up."

So the Jews answered and said to Him, "What sign do You show to us, since You do these things?"

Jesus answered and said to them, "Destroy this temple, and in three days I will raise it up."

Then the Jews said, "It has taken forty-six years to build this temple, and will You raise it up in three days?"

But He was speaking of the temple of His body. Therefore, when He had risen from the dead, His disciples remembered that He had said this to them; and they believed the Scripture and the word which Jesus had said.

What did Jesus see in the temple that upset Him so much?

People selling oxen, sheep, and doves.
Moneychangers.

Can you think of ways that people have made "My Father's house a house of merchandise" today?
Some charities and even Christian ministries get sidetracked and start to worry more about making enough money than about serving God and trusting Him. Televangelists have abused Christ for monetary gain.

_____

_____

Verse 18 describes the demands of the onlookers this way, "What sign do you show us, since You do these things?" Can you explain what gave Jesus the authority to do what He did?
Jesus is the Son of God. It was His house they were abusing.

_____

_____

What did Jesus mean when He referred to Himself as "this temple"?

He was hinting at the fact that He was both the Son of Man and the Son of God. Also that He was about to establish a new covenant that no longer required a physical temple with its sacrifices. Jesus was the one sacrifice that paid the price for all of us. And on another, deeper level, the Holy Spirit now dwells within us. Also, God tells us that our bodies—His creation—should be kept clean and pure (read Romans 12:1–2).

_____

_____

Ravi explains the deeper ramifications of this passage on page 73 of his book where he says, "The Christian does not go to the temple to worship. The Christian takes the temple with him or her. Jesus lifts us beyond the building and pays the human body the highest compliment by making it His dwelling place, the place where He meets with us. Even today He would overturn the tables of those who make it a marketplace for their own lust, greed, and wealth."

How have you allowed Jesus to lift you "beyond the building," so that your focus is on worshipping God and not being in a particular place?

Think about worshipping God while in the car, on a walk, when you wake up or when you go to sleep

---

> There are at least three distinct facets to His answer.
> To see the first facet, we need to look at the *pretext* that the skeptic brought to the verbal exchange. "What sign do You offer for Your authority?" In this challenge, we will see the conflict of faith and reason.
> The second is the *text* with which Jesus responded: "Destroy this temple and in three days I will raise it up." In time, this was going to be the single greatest proof of His claim. Centuries of determination to try to prove Him spurious have only strengthened His proof.
> The last facet of Jesus' answer is the *context* within which He wanted the implication of His message understood. He offered the ultimate miracle by taking that which posed the greatest threat to spiritual inclination and translating it into the center of spirituality. In time, they would recognize that His answer was unique and was sustained by history.
>
> *(Jesus Among Other Gods, pp. 53–54)*

Up to 10 Minutes

Taking It Home

Toward the end of this video segment Ravi quotes Deepak Chopra, who describes the physical body as "a wiggle, a wave, a fluctuation, a convolution, a whirlpool, a localized disturbance in the larger quantum field."

What does Ravi say is misleading about this worldview?

For one thing, if we are all wiggles and waves, then what authority does Mr. Chopra have for sharing this with us? Why should we believe him? But furthermore, in the ministry of Jesus we see examples of real, tangible people encountering Jesus and having their lives radically and completely changed. There is nothing about the crucifixion that could be passed off as a "localized disturbance." Jesus was and is very real, and so are we, His created beings. And it doesn't matter whether you believe it or not, it is still true.

Do you know people who think or talk this way? What new ideas have you learned that would help you share the uniqueness of Jesus' message with them this week?

_____

_____

If you were privileged to grow up in a Christian home, how did your parents convey the notion of the Holy Spirit dwelling within us? How do you understand this unique aspect of Christianity? If you have children, how are you sharing this message with them today?

_____

_____

_____

Some of you may not have been Christians since childhood. If so, before you came to know Christ how did you explain or understand your relationship to the rest of the universe? Why did that make sense at the time? What changed your mind?

_____

_____

_____

As we move into an age filled with relativism and acceptance of all kinds of religions as long as they are not Christianity, what challenges do you think you will encounter compared to the "mood" (as Ravi refers to it) that was prevalent when you grew up?
More resistance to the way we raise our children, criticism about disciplining children, persecution at school, resistance to traditional weddings, prayers, etc.

_____

_____

Be prepared to share your own experience at this point. Your willingness to tell your story will free others to do the same. One participant said, "I was told that when I asked Jesus into my heart, He did come in, and it was called the Holy Spirit."

Close in prayer, referring to the concerns and sharing in this final part of the session.

Lesson 2

"A Taste for the Soul"

Review

In Lesson 1 Ravi addressed the intellectual and spiritual "mood" we see in the world today, where relativism reigns supreme and truth is tossed out the window. As Christians we are called to be "the light of the world" (Matthew 5:14–16), to share our faith with others. However, it can sometimes be hard for others to see how faith in Jesus can stand up to the rigors of reason. Ravi used a unique moment in the ministry of Jesus, when the Pharisees demanded a sign from Jesus to "prove" His divinity (John 2:13–22), to help guide us in this debate.

Warm-up

As we begin Lesson 2, note what Ravi has to say about our hungers:

> "If we were to enumerate all our hungers, we might be surprised at how many legitimate hungers there are. The hunger for truth, the hunger for love, the hunger for knowledge, the hunger to belong.... Some of our individual pursuits may meet some of these hungers... [but] no one thing will meet *all* of these hungers. And furthermore, none can help us know whether the way we fulfill them is legitimate or illegitimate until we feed on the bread of life that Jesus offers. That nourishment defines the legitimacy of all else" (*Jesus Among Other Gods*, p. 86).

Before you watch the second video segment, think about some hungers you have. List at least 10 different "yearnings" you've experienced recently. These could be physical, spiritual, emotional . . .

1. _____
2. _____
3. _____
4. _____
5. _____
6. _____
7. _____
8. _____
9. _____
10. _____

Leader Notes

16-20 Minutes

Make sure you have previewed the video so that you can concentrate on your group's reactions to Ravi's presentation. Review the questions below with the group before you start the video, to prepare them for what they will be hearing and seeing.
Video length: approximately 16 minutes

Do you remember when you were a kid, collecting the toys from inside cereal boxes? One such toy was a "decoder" sheet that was used to decode a secret message on the back of the box. Without the decoder, the message was unreadable—it was a jumble of red and black lines. And although you could make a guess at what it said, you had no way to know for sure. However, as soon as you placed the red decoder sheet over that jumble of lines, the secret message became clear and you could read what it said. Our lives are a jumble of priorities and hungers and desires. We fulfill some and repress others. However, there is no way for us to really know if what we are doing is right. In this lesson we will see that Jesus is the key, the "decoder" for our lives. Only after we have come to Jesus can we begin to decode the secret messages of the meaning of life.

Jonathan Ziman

The Video

Ravi's second video lesson addresses a hunger we all feel deep within our souls—the hunger for meaning and purpose, for something infinite, for something much greater than our day-to-day existence. Ravi will then explain why Jesus is the only one who can fulfill these longings.

As you watch the video, use the outline below to assist you in taking notes:

1. Jesus responds to the people's desire for a miraculous sign, like the manna that Moses provided in the desert.

_____

_____

_____

2. Understanding our hungers.

_____

_____

_____

3. Jesus' provision for the spiritual hunger with which you and I live.

_____

_____

_____

4. Jesus' body and blood mend our broken lives.

_____

_____

_____

5. The uniqueness of the Christian message.

_____

_____

_____

Reviewing the Lesson

Ravi opens the second video session with a quote from John 6, where Jesus says, "Unless you eat the flesh of the Son of Man and drink His blood, you have no life in you" (v. 53).

Most of us have read these words before, and although they may seem clear to us now (after reading commentaries, hearing sermons, going to Sunday school, etc.), can you remember what you thought when you first read them? Similarly, what can you imagine the words must sound like to a nonbeliever?

_____

_____

How would you approach the opportunity to explain the mystery of communion to someone unfamiliar with Christianity? What illustrations or concepts have helped you to explain this important part of our faith to nonbelievers? What methods were the most successful in explaining communion to your kids?
It's an act of worship, of obedience, of remembrance. Jesus wants to be completely a part of us. Jesus wants to commune with us. It's an intimate moment. A meeting place with a loving God. When sharing with kids, focus on communion as a moment where we remember that Jesus died for our sins and rose again out of His great love for us.

_____

_____

One of the illustrations Ravi used in discussing the issue of hungers in the video was this allusion to a comment by D. H. Lawrence: "We often think in life's hungers we are looking for love, that if we find an all-encompassing love of some sort, it would alleviate any sense of loneliness and alienation and be the sum and substance of our answers." But Ravi agreed with Lawrence's assessment that this attitude missed the mark. As Lawrence said, "There is something more than love that we long for."

Leader Notes

Up to 15 Minutes

Most people will probably not be able to recall a time when these words didn't make sense to them. So focus the group on how radical it must have been for the people listening to Jesus. Even today lots of nonbelievers and "unchurched" people have no idea what this means, and hymns about the "blood of Jesus" washing over us can sound bizarre and cannibalistic. Some people reading the Bible for the very first time may even wonder if Jesus was talking about vampirism.

Start with the first of these questions, and use the other two for clarification if necessary.

Reflecting on Lawrence's comment about general attitudes, list some ways in which contemporary society encourages this attitude of looking for an all-encompassing love that will remove all loneliness and alienation.

Romantic movies such as *Titanic,* books, novels, magazine stories, soap operas, TV. Everything today seems to revolve around love and sex being the answers to everything.

Have you ever fallen prey to this kind of thinking? Would you mind sharing how Jesus helped you to see your way out?

Pursuing "love" above all else, or faulty visions of love as portrayed by movies, can damage our relationships with others, and hurt our relationship with God. Any time we seek to satisfy ourselves on our own terms we are taking God out of the picture, and that's a dangerous situation to be in.

In the video Ravi says that Jesus "enables us to understand our hungers."

Based on our study so far, what do you think Ravi means?

Without God in our lives, we are living in sin, and therefore unable to live out the life that God has ordained for us. Jesus enables us to see that what we are really looking for in life is God, not love or food or material wealth.

> "Our greatest hunger, as Jesus described it, is for a consummate relationship that combines the physical and the spiritual, that engenders both awe and love, and that is expressed in celebration and commitment."
>
> (*Jesus Among Other Gods,* p. 9)

At the beginning of this lesson you listed many different types of hungers. Go back and look at those again as you consider the next questions.

In what ways do people try to feed their spiritual needs with physical things?
Suggestions: Perhaps you have single friends who are trying to fulfill their need for the unconditional love of Christ through relationships with people of the opposite sex? Or you feel a restlessness as the Holy Spirit convicts you of sin or is trying to lead you to greater acts of faith, and you try to fill that by buying clothes or changing jobs. We are easily misguided and led astray.

_____

_____

_____

How could someone's attempts to feed some of these hungers in their life perhaps interfere with their relationship with God?
Suggestions: Anytime we are looking for ways to satisfy our own hungers without looking to God first, we are headed down the wrong path. Our actions in and of themselves may not be "wrong" or "bad," but if we are not acting out of obedience to God, then we are opening up the door for temptation to come in.

_____

_____

_____

What suggestions could you give to someone who wants to move beyond physical needs and see that Jesus is calling us into a deeper relationship; that He is there to fill our primary, most fundamental hunger—our spiritual hunger?
Examples: Read your Bible. Pray for God to fill you with a desire to serve Him. Jot down reminders or notes and leave them in prominent places around your house or apartment. If you have a Bible with the words of Jesus printed in red, skim through the book of John and read just the words of Jesus. Pray for God to revive your heart and help you to focus on Him more this week.

_____

_____

_____

Bible Focus
Read John 6:48–58.

"I am the bread of life. Your fathers ate the manna in the wilderness, and are dead. This is the bread which comes down from heaven, that one may eat of it and not die. I am the living bread which came down from heaven. If anyone eats of this bread, he will live forever; and the bread that I shall give is My flesh, which I shall give for the life of the world."

The Jews therefore quarreled among themselves, saying, "How can this Man give us His flesh to eat?"

Then Jesus said to them, "Most assuredly, I say to you, unless you eat the flesh of the Son of Man and drink His blood, you have no life in you. Whoever eats My flesh and drinks My blood has eternal life, and I will raise him up at the last day. For My flesh is food indeed, and My blood is drink indeed. He who eats My flesh and drinks My blood abides in Me, and I in him. As the living Father sent Me, and I live because of the Father, so he who feeds on Me will live because of Me. This is the bread which came down from heaven—not as your fathers ate the manna, and are dead. He who eats this bread will live forever."

What was Jesus referring to when He talked about the people eating "manna in the desert"?

Moses and the Israelites were taught to rely on God for their every need with a visual and physical example of manna/bread from Heaven. It was enough for each day only—symbolic of the grace sufficient for each day that God gives to us now.

_____

_____

_____

What did Jesus say is necessary to "live forever"?

"Eating" His flesh and "drinking" His blood. Obviously this doesn't happen physically, but when we repent and accept Christ into our hearts, the Holy Spirit enters our lives. Metaphorically we are "eating" His flesh when we remember His death for us, and "drinking" His blood when we consider His blood being shed for our sins.

_____

_____

_____

In what ways have you fed on the bread of life and how has it sustained you in ways that real bread cannot?
People who are alive in Christ discover that His presence can be experienced in an amazing variety of circumstances and situations. While certain settings (like church) remain familiar places to spend time with Jesus and be nourished by Him, spiritual growth leads to a continual taking in of Christ's presence. It brings comfort, assurance, peace, joy, meaning, purpose, and the fruit of the Spirit. It's important to remember that having the bread of life does not mean freedom from suffering or a promise of prosperity.

_____

_____

_____

How is the analogy of food and water a perfect example of the relationship Jesus wants us to have with Him?
Food and drink are the basic sustenance of life. We need them both to survive. However, we have no way to store them for very long, so we have to keep consuming more every day. Jesus wants us to yearn for Him on a basic, daily, physical level. And He in turn provides us with spiritual sustenance to make it through each day. So, it expresses the love God has for us, and also the desire that He has for a personal, intimate relationship with us.

_____

_____

_____

Read Matthew 26:26–29.
And as they were eating, Jesus took bread, blessed it and broke it, and gave it to the disciples and said, "Take, eat; this is My body."
Then He took the cup, and gave thanks, and gave it to them, saying, "Drink from it, all of you. For this is My blood of the new covenant, which is shed for many for the remission of sins. But I say to you, I will not drink of this fruit of the vine from now on until that day when I drink it new with you in My Father's kingdom."

What meal were the disciples sharing with Jesus and in what way was it different from other such meals? (Check out Exodus 12 for the primary biblical background.)

The Passover supper was a tradition established in the time of Moses in order to remember how God brought the Jews out of bondage in Egypt and into the Promised Land. It also celebrates God's faithfulness while the Jews wandered in the desert and expresses a hope for the coming of the Messiah (see Exodus 12). Jesus fulfilled this hope for a Messiah and brings us into the "Promised Land" of salvation.

_____

_____

_____

What do *you* think Jesus meant when He said, "Take, eat; this is My body" (Matthew 26:26)?

_____

_____

_____

What "covenant" was Jesus talking about? What clues are in the passage?

There are many covenants made between God and His people in the Old Testament, but Jesus was a "new" covenant—a new sign of God's promises to His people (see Hebrews 8–10). Jesus is a sign and a symbol of God's amazing steadfast love for us. Note that the covenant has a direct connection with the forgiveness of sins.

_____

_____

_____

Compare the sacrifices that the Israelites were required to make to atone for their sins with the sacrifice that Jesus made. How did He abolish the need for such animal sacrifices once and for all? (Consult Hebrews 10:1–18 for insights into the differences between the old sacrifices and Jesus' death.)

Animal sacrifices were the only way to avoid God's judgment—a death was required to "pay" for the sins of the people. Jesus, being free from sin, was able to pay for all our sins with His death.

_____

_____

_____

Read John 4:5–15.

So He came to a city of Samaria which is called Sychar, near the plot of ground that Jacob gave to his son Joseph. Now Jacob's well was there. Jesus therefore, being wearied from His journey, sat thus by the well. It was about the sixth hour. A woman of Samaria came to draw water. Jesus said to her, "Give Me a drink." For His disciples had gone away into the city to buy food.

Then the woman of Samaria said to Him, "How is it that You, being a Jew, ask a drink from me, a Samaritan woman?" For Jews have no dealings with Samaritans.

Jesus answered and said to her, "If you knew the gift of God, and who it is who says to you, 'Give Me a drink,' you would have asked Him, and He would have given you living water."

The woman said to Him, "Sir, You have nothing to draw with, and the well is deep. Where then do You get that living water? Are You greater than our father Jacob, who gave us the well, and drank from it himself, as well as his sons and his livestock?"

Jesus answered and said to her, "Whoever drinks of this water will thirst again, but whoever drinks of the water that I shall give him will never thirst. But the water that I shall give him will become in him a fountain of water springing up into everlasting life."

The woman said to Him, "Sir, give me this water, that I may not thirst, nor come here to draw."

What types of hunger did this woman probably have?
Suggestions: Thirsty for water, yearning for love (she had many husbands), seeking spiritual healing and a sense of purpose and direction (she asks for the living water).

_____ ·
_____
_____

Why do you think this interaction between a woman and Jesus makes such a memorable chapter in the Bible?
Suggestions: There are many of us who long for deeper satisfaction than what the world provides, and yet we often feel unworthy to ask God for help. This interaction reinforces the message that Jesus came to save us all, the dirty as well as the clean, Jews and Gentiles alike. We are never too unworthy to turn to God and ask for help.

_____
_____
_____

Leader Notes

What situations in your life can you think of when you decided not to talk to someone about God, just because it was socially not acceptable?
Suggestions: Perhaps talking to someone of another religion, someone deep in sin, someone far away from God, etc. Be bold and share your faith with everyone—the message of Jesus is especially for those who seem farthest away from God.

_____

_____

_____

What do you find amazing about Jesus asking this woman for a drink and how does it model many of God's interactions with us?
Jesus initiated the conversation with this woman— He called out to her. God is calling out to us as well. Are we going to respond?

_____

_____

_____

Taking It Home
What have been some of your most vivid experiences during communion? Take some time to think about what this act means to you. Write down your thoughts here, and next time you go to communion at church, think about what this act signifies.

_____

_____

_____

What suggestions could you offer someone who wanted to make sure communion becomes more than just a routine in their spiritual life?
Because Paul places an emphasis on preparation and self-examination (1 Corinthians 11:17–34), many people make it a point to anticipate communion with personal disciplines. Some people fast, some give special attention to confession of sins, and others pray during or before communion.

_____

_____

_____

Ravi comments in the video, "We are broken away from God. We are broken away from one another. We are even broken from ourselves. Life is disconnected....[but Jesus] gives us the insight of what it means to be whole, and we relive life the way it was intended to be lived out."

In what ways are we "broken from ourselves"?

_____

_____

_____

What do you think is the need or secret desire behind the people in our world who want to see themselves as being divine or containing the divine within them? (Ravi quotes Deepak Chopra talking about "the unfolding of the divinity within us.")
The focus here is not so much on the gurus or odd people who declare themselves to be messiahs, but on those everyday people who are "searching for the goddess or god within." Most often this attempt to define divinity as something that is attainable (as is often the case in Hinduism and New Age religions) serves as an affirmation that they aren't "bad" people. It helps people to get over the burden of sin they feel in their lives. It also means they can avoid having to be held accountable for their actions, or having to accept the presence of one God.

_____

_____

_____

Possible comment note: "Be all that you can be" used to be the advertising motto of the US Army. Without Jesus though, even the Army cannot enable us to be everything that God intended for us to be. In this respect we are "broken" from ourselves, separated from the person that God created. Even after we have been "saved" we may lack self-confidence and not realize or accept the gifts God has given each of us as members of the body. This can be manifested in not being content with who we are or striving to be someone else. These all leave us disconnected and disjointed.

In the broken relationships you may see around you, how can you share the "wholeness" that Christ brings to your life?
Christ enables us to discover purpose and meaning in life. Before Christ we are dead in sin. After Christ we are alive in Him. Life may still beat us down, but we are now at a point where we can be open and honest with others who are suffering. We can let them know that they are not alone. Support them and pray with them. Share how God brought you through similar events. The church is filled with those who have turned away from lives of great sin (such as alcoholism or drugs) and can now minister to those who are still stuck in those sins. Christ is the one who enables that.

_____

_____

_____

"Communion" is one of several unique aspects of Christianity. There is nothing like it in any of the other major world religions.

Hinduism, for example, stresses union with "the divine." There is no single God to have a relationship with. Instead, to quote Deepak Chopra, the focus is on "the unfolding of the divinity within us."

Muslims are at the other end of the spectrum. Although they believe in God, He is so totally transcendent that His nearness in a personal relationship is lost. The separation is permanent, so there can be no communion.

Jesus came to bridge that gap and bring us the "bread of life"—the only food that can nourish our souls and bring us into a right relationship with God. Have you partaken of this heavenly feast?

Take a moment to ask the group about people they know who need to meet Christ in the way you have been discussing. Invite them to pray for those friends by name. As you end the prayer time, ask God to help each of you be aware of ways in which He may want you to participate in bringing the gospel to those people.

Lesson 3

"Is God the Source of My Suffering?"

Review

In Lesson 1 Ravi addressed the mood of relativism that is so pervasive in society today. In Lesson 2 Ravi explained that Jesus is absolutely the only one who can fulfill our deep spiritual needs. In Lesson 3 Ravi will discuss a question that has plagued mankind for thousands of years—"Is God the source of my suffering?" As we shall see, the question was certainly on the minds of the people in Jesus' day.

Warm-up

Before watching the third video segment, think about some times you have experienced suffering and persecution in your life. List below some of the initial reactions you remember experiencing during those times of trouble:

1. _____

_____

_____

2. _____

_____

_____

3. _____

_____

_____

4. _____

_____

_____

In what ways did you connect your suffering with God?

_____

_____

_____

Ask the group to review the task and questions below on their own for a minute or two, and then discuss them briefly. If they are eager to talk, encourage them to save extended comments until after the video. Up to 5 Minutes

How did you justify and work through your anger, sadness, or doubt toward God?
Although some people may be reserved or ashamed and not want to share on this question, if we are honest almost everyone has experienced some form of anger toward God at some point in their lives. And quite often it is related to suffering we are going through, or confusion about God's plan in our lives. This can be a good opportunity to start thinking about times of pain in our lives and how we reacted to that pain. However angry, upset, or confused we may have been, God's patience, love, and mercy endure forever. Someone in the group may benefit from hearing about struggles that others have overcome.

_____

_____

_____

Ask someone to be prepared to read this letter for the group as an introduction to the video.
25 Minutes

Make sure you have previewed the video so that you can concentrate on your group's reactions to Ravi's presentation. Encourage the group to read over the outline points below before starting the video.
Video length: approximately 22 minutes

The Video
If you have a copy of *Jesus Among Other Gods*, read the letter that is printed at the beginning of Chapter 5 before watching the video. Then, using the outline below to help you focus on the key points in the video, jot down some notes in the space provided. These will assist you as you work through the rest of the lesson.

1. The skeptic's question:

_____

_____

_____

2. The contradiction inherent in the skeptic's point of view:

_____

_____

_____

3. The atheist's explanation of suffering:

_____

_____

_____

4. The contradiction inherent in the atheist's point of view:

_____

_____

_____

5. The pantheist's explanation of suffering:
   a. The Buddhist says:

_____

_____

_____

   b. The Hindu says:

_____

_____

_____

6. The common ground between Buddhism and Hinduism:

_____

_____

_____

7. Contradiction/philosophical problem:

_____

_____

_____

8. What the Bible really says about the problem of suffering and evil:

_____

_____

_____

9. Summary statements and other notes:

_____

_____

_____

Reviewing the Lesson

Ravi begins his discussion of suffering with a look at John 9:1–11, where Jesus and the disciples encounter a man who has been blind since birth.

Now as Jesus passed by, He saw a man who was blind from birth. And His disciples asked Him, saying, "Rabbi, who sinned, this man or his parents, that he was born blind?"
Jesus answered, "Neither this man nor his parents sinned, but that the works of God should be revealed in him. I must work the works of Him who sent Me while it is day; the night is coming when no one can work. As long as I am in the world, I am the light of the world."
When He had said these things, He spat on the ground and made clay with the saliva; and He anointed the eyes of the blind man with the clay. And He said to him, "Go, wash in the pool of Siloam" (which is translated, Sent). So he went and washed, and came back seeing.
Therefore the neighbors and those who previously had seen that he was blind said, "Is not this he who sat and begged?"

Up to 10 Minutes

Some said, "This is he."
Others said, "He is like him."
He said, "I am he."
Therefore they said to him, "How were your eyes opened?"
He answered and said, "A Man called Jesus made clay and anointed my eyes and said to me, 'Go to the pool of Siloam and wash.' So I went and washed, and I received sight."

The disciples, already having learned a great deal from Jesus, hope to get a definitive answer from Him regarding the cause of this man's suffering. It was common in Jewish tradition to explain all suffering as a punishment for some specific sin, so they want to find out if Jesus agrees with that or not. However, Jesus gives them an answer they probably weren't expecting— "Neither this man nor his parents sinned, but that the works of God might be revealed in him."

In how many different ways do you think the disciples might have responded to this statement?
Surprise, confusion, frustration, disbelief.... They probably didn't really understand what He was saying.

_____

_____

_____

What do *you* think Jesus was saying?
Some people say that the healing and teaching were meant to point to something bigger, i.e., we are all blind spiritually, and it requires the work of God in our lives to "heal" us. Jesus is also shifting the disciples' focus away from the blind man and his suffering to the glory and power of God. He was not saying that God made this man blind and left him like that for 40 years in pain just to make a point to the disciples. But Jesus was able to take something awful and make it beautiful, and that's what He does to our lives as well.

_____

_____

_____

Remind your group that the disciples (like us) were looking for a cause/effect answer—which was reinforced by Jesus' recent teachings that we are all held accountable for our sins. The disciples hadn't considered that another reason for the blind man's suffering might have nothing to do with the him at all, but the bigger picture of God's glory.

How would you apply Jesus' words and actions to someone who is suffering right now?

First of all, pray. Jesus healed the blind man "so that the glory of God might be displayed in his life." We can't display the glory of God unless we are acting in accordance to His will, which means praying first and foremost. Any time you share with someone who is suffering it is also important to be sensitive to their pain. On the one hand, one shouldn't wallow in depression, but on the other hand it is often necessary to grieve and cry and be sad before the healing can begin. All of that said, this passage directs us to focus on God and how we might glorify Him during our times of struggle. It may be that He can use our suffering to minister to others who are suffering.

_____

_____

_____

How does Jesus' explanation regarding the blind man help you understand better your own past or present experiences of suffering?

God makes good out of bad. The biggest evidence of this is the cross, but it happens on a smaller scale in our day-to-day lives as well. There is a great comfort and even peace when you realize that sometimes there is a purpose outside of your suffering— perhaps it will help bring someone to Christ, or help you comfort a fellow believer.

_____

_____

_____

All too frequently we hear people say, "There cannot be an all-powerful, all-loving God because of the presence of evil in the world." Ravi responds to this philosophical outlook by showing that the skeptic unwittingly acknowledges the presence of God by making such a statement.

How would you approach the illogical basis of the skeptic's belief? Write in your own words how you would explain that by demanding an explanation for the presence of evil in this world, one automatically assumes the presence of a moral universe and a moral being as its first cause.

To deny the presence of God because of the presence of evil in this world is to say that there are objective values such as right and wrong. After all, how else do you judge "evil" and "good"? And if there is some kind of objective moral order, where does that come from? The only reasonable answer is that it comes from someone who is moral and just—God.

_____

_____

_____

Encourage the group to take some time to go over their answers to the question above (regarding the logical problems with the skeptic's explanation for evil) with the rest of your group, until they feel confident in being able to explain this to a nonbeliever or someone who is asking about Christianity.

Remind the group to think about/discuss the notion of "free will." If a person could only decide to do right, could they be in any sense, free?

It is crucial to be able to explain why the presence of suffering and evil do not disprove the existence of God.

In the video Ravi explains how some atheists challenge the idea of God with the question, "How come God didn't make us as beings who can only do good?"

How does he answer this question?
To have made us all "good" would have been to make us like robots. Forced love is empty. Only love that comes freely is genuine.

_____

_____

_____

Adherents to Hinduism and Buddhism both believe in reincarnation, that "every birth is a rebirth, and every birth is a payment for the previous life." However, despite their agreement about what happens when we die, they have distinct views regarding what happens while we are alive.

Hinduism:
1. What we see and feel and experience is not "real" at all, it is "transitory" and impermanent. Therefore, when we experience suffering it also is an "impermanent" and "transitory" state.

2. Since the world we live in isn't "real," we are in the process of struggling toward what is real. _Hinduism Today_ describes it thus: "Hindus believe that the soul reincarnates, evolving through many births until all karmas have been resolved, and moksha, spiritual

3. A common analogy in Hinduism is that we are actors in a play, reciting lines, acting out roles, "playing our part." Eventually the play will end and the curtain will be drawn. At that point "we will find the permanence of one ultimate reality behind it all."

Buddhism:

1. What we see and feel and experience is very real. Suffering is a part of that reality.

2. Since the world we live in is so very real, we need to try and shed that reality and move toward a "higher state" where we see the impermanence of things. Suffering will hold no meaning at this point.

[1]http://www.himalayanacademy.com/basics/point/index.html

Leader Notes

Read the main points of Buddhist and Hindu philosophies regarding the concept of suffering (see the sidebar) and keep in mind what you learned from Ravi. What have been your experiences with people of these faiths? Based on their beliefs, how do you think they would try to comfort someone during a time of suffering? Or, how would they respond to comfort?

_____

_____

_____

If you haven't had any contact with people of these beliefs, which of the following do you think you would have the hardest time doing?
Explaining your own beliefs?
Talking about Jesus?
Talking about what is "real" and what isn't?

_____

_____

A good exercise here may be to try some role-playing exercises. This will help people realize where their comfort-zone ends and where they will need God to help them minister to those in another culture/religion.

Leader Notes

Assign each of the first three passages to a small group and have them read the passage and answer the questions. Then have each small group present a summary of their discussion to the whole group. Keep this relatively short.
Read and study Matthew 26:36–46 with the entire group.
Up to 15 minutes

It is important to stress that Jesus, as God, knew the storm would occur and was planning on using this as a real-life teaching experience. The storm was in His control, and His miracle was planned ahead of time, not merely a response to something that caught Him off-guard.

Bible Focus
Read Mark 4:35–41, an account of when Jesus calmed the storm.

On the same day, when evening had come, He said to them, "Let us cross over to the other side." Now when they had left the multitude, they took Him along in the boat as He was. And other little boats were also with Him. And a great windstorm arose, and the waves beat into the boat, so that it was already filling. But He was in the stern, asleep on a pillow.
And they awoke Him and said to Him, "Teacher, do You not care that we are perishing?"
Then He arose and rebuked the wind, and said to the sea, "Peace, be still!" And the wind ceased and there was a great calm. But He said to them, "Why are you so fearful? How is it that you have no faith?"
And they feared exceedingly, and said to one another, "Who can this be, that even the wind and the sea obey Him!"

Who suggested that they should get in the boats and cross the lake?
Jesus.

_____

_____

_____

What was Jesus doing during the storm?
Sleeping. He was allowing the disciples to fend for themselves—letting them reach a point where they had to make a decision about what to do and whom to turn to. He had to allow them to get to a low point in order for them to see where their faith was.

_____

_____

_____

What happened when the disciples woke Jesus up?
He calmed the storm and began His teaching lesson. He asked them why they were afraid. They had the Son of God sitting in the boat with them! Was it really going to sink? Yet the disciples were still full of fear. He makes this a direct point by asking, "Do you still have no faith?" It is significant that the moment we call on God, He brings us peace, calming our fears. But, we must seek Him first. He is waiting for us to ask for help.

_____

_____

_____

How was Jesus' perspective on the situation different from the disciples'?
They were sure the boat was about to sink. They were almost right— "it was nearly swamped"—but the boat stayed afloat! From the perspective of the disciples, all hope was lost and they were going to drown. But once again, their perspective was too narrow, and they couldn't see beyond their own fears. It's so easy to get caught up in how bad our own situation is that we forget that God is bigger than it all. He didn't just create us, He created the whole universe. That puts a slightly different perspective on our own earthly trials and tribulations.

What lessons can be applied to life from this passage?
Times of suffering and difficulty do not mean that we are outside the will of God. And likewise, doing the will of God doesn't shield us from trials and tribulations. Jesus is with us always, even when it seems like we are about to go under. And assuming that we got in the right boat, headed in the right direction, to begin with, Jesus will help us make it through.

Read 2 Corinthians 4:7–12.
But we have this treasure in earthen vessels, that the excellence of the power may be of God and not of us. We are hard pressed on every side, yet not crushed; we are perplexed, but not in despair; persecuted, but not forsaken; struck down, but not destroyed—always carrying about in the body the dying of the Lord Jesus, that the life of Jesus also may be manifested in our body. For we who live are always delivered to death for Jesus' sake, that the life of Jesus also may be manifested in our mortal flesh. So then death is working in us, but life in you.

What conclusions do you draw from Paul's use of "earthen vessels" to describe Christians?
This offers a great picture of how fragile, weak, and brittle we can be. The fact that God places the treasure of eternal life into such containers becomes a tribute to His power.

From your own experiences or observations, what kinds of circumstances do you think Paul had in mind when he wrote of being "hard pressed on every side"?

_____

_____

_____

Paul knew suffering in his own life. What is his message of hope for us?
Suffering and persecution will come, but we are "more than conquerors" in Jesus Christ (Romans 8:37). Jesus Christ suffered crucifixion and death, BUT He rose again to bring us life, and to bring meaning and purpose to our lives. His sacrifice gives us reason to live.

_____

_____

_____

Based on this passage and your own experiences, how would you approach sharing the message of eternal life in Jesus with someone this week?

_____

_____

_____

Read Psalm 22.
My God, My God, why have You forsaken Me?
Why are You so far from helping Me,
And from the words of My groaning?
O My God, I cry in the daytime, but You do not hear;
And in the night season, and am not silent.

But You are holy,
Enthroned in the praises of Israel.
Our fathers trusted in You;
They trusted, and You delivered them.
They cried to You, and were delivered;
They trusted in You, and were not ashamed.

But I am a worm, and no man;
A reproach of men, and despised by the people.
All those who see Me ridicule Me;
They shoot out the lip, they shake the head, saying,
"He trusted in the LORD, let Him rescue Him;
Let Him deliver Him, since He delights in Him!"

But You are He who took Me out of the womb;
You made Me trust while on My mother's breasts.
I was cast upon You from birth.
From My mother's womb
You have been My God.
Be not far from Me,

For trouble is near;
For there is none to help.

Many bulls have surrounded Me;
Strong bulls of Bashan have encircled Me.
They gape at Me with their mouths,
Like a raging and roaring lion.

I am poured out like water,
And all My bones are out of joint;
My heart is like wax;
It has melted within Me.
My strength is dried up like a potsherd,
And My tongue clings to My jaws;
You have brought Me to the dust of death.

For dogs have surrounded Me;
The congregation of the wicked has enclosed Me.
They pierced My hands and My feet;
I can count all My bones.
They look and stare at Me.
They divide My garments among them,
And for My clothing they cast lots.

But You, O Lord, do not be far from Me;
O My Strength, hasten to help Me!
Deliver Me from the sword,
My precious life from the power of the dog.
Save Me from the lion's mouth
And from the horns of the wild oxen!

You have answered Me.

I will declare Your name to My brethren;
In the midst of the assembly I will praise You.
You who fear the Lord, praise Him!
All you descendants of Jacob, glorify Him,
And fear Him, all you offspring of Israel!
For He has not despised nor abhorred the affliction of the afflicted;
Nor has He hidden His face from Him;
But when He cried to Him, He heard.

My praise shall be of You in the great assembly;
I will pay My vows before those who fear Him.
The poor shall eat and be satisfied;
Those who seek Him will praise the Lord.
Let your heart live forever!

All the ends of the world
Shall remember and turn to the Lord,
And all the families of the nations
Shall worship before You.
For the kingdom is the Lord's,
And He rules over the nations.

All the prosperous of the earth
Shall eat and worship;
All those who go down to the dust

Shall bow before Him,
Even he who cannot keep himself alive.

A posterity shall serve Him.
It will be recounted of the Lᴏʀᴅ to the next generation,
They will come and declare His righteousness to a people who
will be born,
That He has done this.

Check or underline some of the verses that emphasize just how deep David's suffering is:
1, 2, 6, 7, 12–18

What phrase (or phrases) represent the turning point in this psalm?
Verse 19— "But you, O Lᴏʀᴅ. . . ." It's the moment where David shifts his focus from himself and his struggles to the Lord and His power and glory. It also echoes the "but" in the 2 Corinthians passage we just studied. There was a time for lamenting, but also a time to praise God despite his circumstances. (Read Ecclesiastes 3:1–8).

What reasons does David give for saying that we should praise the Lord?
Verse 24— "For He has not despised nor abhorred the affliction of the afflicted; nor has He hidden His face from Him; but when He cried to Him, He heard." Also, 25–31, God loves us and is waiting to help us in our times of trouble.

What from your own experience are the results of praising the Lord?
Being uplifted in spirit and mind, taking your focus off the problems of this world and looking to God. Also it results in the pleasure of glorifying God and being obedient to Him. This all encourages trust and builds faith which furthers God's ability to use us and which in turn will result in blessings for us. It's a positive feedback loop.

Read Matthew 26:36–46.

Then Jesus came with them to a place called Gethsemane, and said to the disciples, "Sit here while I go and pray over there." And He took with Him Peter and the two sons of Zebedee, and He began to be sorrowful and deeply distressed. Then He said to them, "My soul is exceedingly sorrowful, even to death. Stay here and watch with Me."

He went a little farther and fell on His face, and prayed, saying, "O My Father, if it is possible, let this cup pass from Me; nevertheless, not as I will, but as You will."

Then He came to the disciples and found them asleep, and said to Peter, "What? Could you not watch with Me one hour? Watch and pray, lest you enter into temptation. The spirit indeed is willing, but the flesh is weak."

Again, a second time, He went away and prayed, saying, "O My Father, if this cup cannot pass away from Me unless I drink it, Your will be done." And He came and found them asleep again, for their eyes were heavy.

So He left them, went away again, and prayed the third time, saying the same words. Then He came to His disciples and said to them, "Are you still sleeping and resting? Behold, the hour is at hand, and the Son of Man is being betrayed into the hands of sinners. Rise, let us be going. See, My betrayer is at hand."

Also look at the corresponding passage in Luke 22:39–46.

Coming out, He went to the Mount of Olives, as He was accustomed, and His disciples also followed Him. When He came to the place, He said to them, "Pray that you may not enter into temptation."

And He was withdrawn from them about a stone's throw, and He knelt down and prayed, saying, "Father, if it is Your will, take this cup away from Me; nevertheless not My will, but Yours, be done." Then an angel appeared to Him from heaven, strengthening Him. And being in agony, He prayed more earnestly. Then His sweat became like great drops of blood falling down to the ground.

When He rose up from prayer, and had come to His disciples, He found them sleeping from sorrow. Then He said to them, "Why do you sleep? Rise and pray, lest you enter into temptation."

What was Jesus feeling when He entered the garden of Gethsemane?

Acute sadness, loneliness, and fearfulness regarding what was about to come. We encounter these emotions as well when we first hit a time of trial and suffering.

What did Jesus do?

He prayed. He focused on His desire that the Lord's will be done, and God strengthened Him to be able to endure the time ahead.

Summarize Jesus' prayer in your own words:
Father, what's going to happen next is so awful and humiliating and painful I don't think I can handle it (reminiscent of the disciples' boat being "nearly swamped"). Please, if there's any possibility of your will being accomplished in a different manner, let me know. I don't know if I can do this. Help me to do your will Father, whatever that entails.

List some phrases from the passages you just read that emphasize how deep His suffering was:
Luke 22:44, Matthew 26:38, Psalm 22:1

How did God answer Jesus' prayers?

Luke 22:43—an angel strengthened Him. But otherwise God said "no" to Jesus' requests. The bottom line is that God's will was done. However, He did give Jesus the strength to endure.

How could someone use these passages to comfort a friend who is feeling alone in their suffering?

Jesus knows your pain! He knows your anguish and suffering and loneliness. But in the midst of it all, He chose to do God's will anyway. Is that the path that you choose? Or do you simply ask for the pain to be taken away? Instead, ask the Lord for the ability to endure whatever lies ahead, and for the strength to continue on whatever path God has chosen for you.

Taking It Home

Ravi's Six Biblical Concepts on Suffering

1. God is the author of life.
2. There is a script to that life if God is the author.
3. There is a purpose for that script that goes beyond our immediate day-to-day happiness.
4. There is a moral justification given to us by God of why evil exists.
5. The ultimate struggle with evil is within, not externally.
6. Evil may not be the most difficult question of all.

Ravi says, in response to the pantheistic belief of reincarnation, that the Christian viewpoint is, "There is a life that is lived, a culminating moment, and then that time spent in eternity either with God or separated from God. There is no reincarnational motif in the Christian Scriptures" (from the video, *Jesus Among Other Gods*).

Considering that there is only one life that we live, at this point in time how is your walk with God going? How would you describe your level of satisfaction with the life you have lived so far?

_____

_____

_____

What steps could you take in the next several days that you know would help you to live a life "holy and pleasing to God" (Romans 12:1)?

_____

_____

_____

This answer might be very specific for those who have strayed from the path. And for those who are walking with Jesus the answers may be very general. Encourage those who are specific about changes in their lives. Offer to set up prayer partners to hold people accountable to following God's Word.

We live in a fallen, sinful world where we encounter great difficulties and trouble on a day-to-day basis.

Think about the people with various health-related problems or emotional struggles that are on your prayer list right now. Note some of the details below:

_____

_____

_____

Leader Notes

Again, if you discuss this in the group remember to be sensitive to their struggles and pain. These answers will vary because each person is unique before God and will need a different approach. Look at how Jesus talked with the woman at the well, compared to Nicodemus, compared to Bartimaeus or the rich young ruler. There are no pat answers you can give when someone is in pain.

Encourage group members to incorporate worship into their daily prayers.

Pick one or two people from your prayer list (above) and explain how you would talk to them about their suffering in relation to God.

Ravi says that "worship is what binds together all of the various propensities of the human heart and brings it into a composite expression of what life is intended to be." (See also 1 Corinthians 10:31 and Psalm 73:25–26.)

List some specific ways that you can make worship a part of your daily walk with Christ.
Sing in the car! Pray in the train! There are many ways to make worship part of your daily routine. Using a concordance or Bible software do a search for all the instances where God says "I am...." Then praise God for His attributes every time you pray (along the lines of the "ACTS" method of praying—Adoration, Confession, Thanksgiving, Supplication).

Ravi describes the cross as the place where "ultimate goodness" and "ultimate evil" converge. It represents at the same time both "the ultimate goodness, the grace and mercy of God, and ultimate evil, where humanity rejected this goodness."

Why is it important to understand evil as well as goodness, hell as well as heaven, demons as well as angels?
You can't understand the great meaning of what Jesus did for us without first seeing how sinful we are. The power of the cross is limited if we ignore the evil that put Jesus on it. You can't have the resurrection without the death first. Furthermore, you can't understand fully the sin in your own life and your need for redemption without accepting and understanding what Satan did to bring sin into the world.

What dangers are faced by those who discount the existence of evil, hell, demons, and Satan?
It's a half-truth—a made-up world that denies our own sinfulness and need for God.

_____

_____

Toward the end of Chapter Five in *Jesus Among Other Gods*, Ravi explains the source of suffering in this world:

> "The problem of evil has ultimately one source. It is the resistance to God's holiness that blanketed all of creation. It is a mystery because we are engulfed in it—spiritual blindness. And there is ultimately only one antidote, the glorious display of God at work within a human soul, bringing about His work of restoration. That transformation tenderizes the heart to become part of the solution and not part of the problem. Such a transformation begins at the cross" (pp. 137–38).

Returning to the questions that opened this lesson, has God been the source of your suffering? Ravi emphasizes that evil and suffering stem from the fact that we are "disconnected" from God. In your deepest times of suffering, what specific steps could you take to connect back with God?
Read the Bible, pray, fellowship with other believers, set up prayer partners. Put your sins and your desires at God's feet and accept Jesus' atonement for your transgressions. Lean on Jesus as a friend who has endured great suffering and will provide you with much strength.

_____

_____

Suffering and Evil

It is important to distinguish between the source of suffering and the source of evil. The source of all evil is resistance to God's will. This is what caused Satan to fall, and what in turn caused our own fall. Suffering stems from this initial state of fallenness, but most often it falls into one of the following four categories:

1. The direct consequence of specific sin in our life. There are many examples in the Bible, but broadly stated, this is the law of cause and effect. Even though we live under grace, there are always consequences for our sin. Adam and Eve were the first to experience this, and David is another prominent example.

2. The direct consequence of specific sin in someone else's life. Sometimes our suffering may be the result of someone else's sin. Uriah did nothing wrong, but he was killed as a result of David's sin.

3. Failure to heed warnings or take precautions. The Bible is full of direction and guidance for our lives. From the Ten Commandments to Proverbs to the Sermon on the Mount, God has provided plenty of instruction to help us avoid certain types of suffering and to lead a life that is pleasing to Him.

4. The work of Satan, as allowed by God. Job is the main example of this kind of spiritual warfare.

As you close in prayer, invite group members to pray for those people whose suffering they just considered. Ask God to make your group agents that carry God's healing and comforting message into the world.

Lesson 4

"Is There a Gardener?"

Review

So far in this study we have looked at three questions that were posed to Jesus, and the unique way in which He responded to each of them.

In Lesson 1 we examined Jesus' response to the Pharisees in John 2:18–19. They asked Jesus, "What miraculous sign can you show us to prove your authority to do all this?" And Jesus responded, "Destroy this temple, and I will raise it again in three days." His answer was completely beyond anything they could comprehend at the time.

In Lesson 2 Ravi helped us understand John 6:30, where the people again demanded, "What miraculous sign then will you give that we may see it and believe you? What will you do? Our forefathers ate the manna in the desert; as it is written: 'He gave them bread from heaven to eat.'" And this time Jesus gave them an answer that goes beyond their physical need for food and instead answers their deep spiritual longings. He said, "I am the bread of life. He who comes to me will never go hungry, and he who believes in me will never be thirsty" (v. 35).

And finally, in Lesson 3 we looked at John 9:1–3, where Jesus healed a blind man. The disciples, trying to understand the suffering that is so present in the world, ask Jesus, "Rabbi, who sinned, this man or his parents, that he was born blind?" Jesus responds, "Neither this man nor his parents sinned, but that the works of God should be revealed in him." It was such a radical answer for the disciples that they never quite grasped what He was talking about until after His resurrection.

But Jesus was more than a "deep thinker" or powerful philosopher. He didn't just "talk the talk," but He "walked the walk" as well. And now, in Lesson 4, Ravi will lead us to what is arguably the most unique and special part of Christianity—the crucifixion and resurrection of Jesus Christ. For without these two events, everything else about Jesus Christ becomes empty and meaningless. As Paul says, if Christ weren't resurrected, then "we are to be pitied more than all men" (1 Corinthians 15:17–18).

**Take a few moments to read or paraphrase the following review for your group.
2 minutes.**

As we have seen in the lessons so far, Jesus is the only person in history who addresses the biggest questions in life— "Why am I here?" "What is my purpose in life?" "Why is there suffering?" Jesus is the one who brings direction. Jesus is the only one who enables us to understand ourselves and our relationship with God.

This is the last lesson, so you want to start focusing in on the unique nature of Jesus Christ. Try to draw out or focus on aspects that were covered in previous lessons.

Warm-up

How have you responded to the question, "How do you know if God exists if you have never seen Him?"

Try to focus people on other intangibles such as, How do you know you love your children? How do you know your parents love you? Your spouse?

_____

_____

_____

How would you respond to the statement, "Christianity is a crutch"?

Perhaps for some people it may be considered a crutch, but that is very short sighted. If you've got a broken arm, you go see a doctor. If you're drowning at sea and someone throws you a life preserver, you grab hold! We are all dead in our sins, and Jesus came to offer us a way out—the only way out. It is foolishness to ignore His gift and try to make it under our own steam. But the message of Jesus goes beyond that; the Gospel presents a true description of reality and an eminently credible depiction of our nature and purpose.

_____

_____

_____

Based on your own understanding so far, how is a crucified and risen Savior unique to Christianity?

Out of all the "saviors" and "prophets" and "holy men" this world has seen, Jesus was the only one who claimed to be God and Man at the same time. He was the only one to fulfill all the Old Testament prophecies regarding the Messiah. He was the only one to live a sinless life. He was the only one who predicted His own death and resurrection. He was the only one who was actually resurrected from the dead. He was the only one who claimed to be dying for our sins. There are more, but this should be enough to get people started.

_____

_____

_____

The Video

This is the last video segment in this study, and Ravi structures it around four "gardens," that represent four different aspects of Jesus Christ and His ministry.

As you watch the video, use the outline below to assist you in taking notes:

1. Initial thoughts about the first garden parable:

_____

_____

_____

Leader Notes

25 Minutes

Make sure you have previewed the video so that you can concentrate on your group's reactions to Ravi's presentation. Base your brief introduction on your own responses in viewing Ravi's conclusions to the series. Video length: approximately 24 minutes.

2. Initial thoughts about the second garden parable:

_____

_____

_____

3. Thoughts about the third "garden":

_____

_____

_____

4. Thoughts about the fourth "garden":

_____

_____

_____

5. How is Jesus "more than a gardener"?

_____

_____

_____

Reviewing the Lesson

Ravi frames this last lesson in the series in reference to two different parables, one written by two naturalist philosophers, and the other written by a Christian philosopher.

Have the group read the two parables silently and answer the questions that follow on their own. Discuss briefly before moving on to the "garden" section. Up to 15 minutes

Parable 1

Once upon a time two explorers came upon a clearing in a jungle. In the clearing growing side by side were many flowers and many weeds. One of the explorers exclaimed, "Some gardener must tend this plot!" So they pitched their tents and set a watch. But though they waited several days no gardener was seen.

"Perhaps he is an invisible gardener!" they thought. So they set up a barbed-wire fence and connected it to electricity. They even patrolled the garden with bloodhounds, for they remembered that H. G. Wells's "Invisible Man" could be both smelt and touched though he could not be seen. But no sounds ever suggested that someone had received an electric shock. No movements of the wire ever betrayed an invisible climber. The bloodhounds never alerted them to the presence of any other in the garden than themselves. Yet, still the believer between them was convinced that there was indeed a gardener.

"There must be a gardener, invisible, intangible, insensible to electric shocks, a gardener who has no scent and makes no sound, a gardener who comes secretly to look after the garden which he loves."

At last the skeptical explorer despaired, "But what remains of your original assertion? Just how does what you call an invisible, intangible, eternally elusive gardener differ from an imaginary gardener or even from no gardener at all?"

By Anthony Flew and John Wisdom

Parable 2

Once upon a time, two explorers came upon a clearing in the jungle. A man was there, pulling weeds, applying fertilizer, and trimming branches. The man turned to the explorers and introduced himself as the royal gardener. One explorer shook his hand and exchanged pleasantries. The other ignored the gardener and turned away.

"There can be no gardener in this part of the jungle," he said. "This must be some trick. Someone is trying to discredit our secret findings."

They pitched camp. And every day the gardener arrived to tend the garden. Soon it was bursting with perfectly arranged blooms. But the skeptical explorer insisted, "He's only doing it because we are here—to fool us into thinking that this is a royal garden."

One day the gardener took them to the royal palace and introduced the explorers to a score of officials who verified the gardener's status. Then the skeptic tried a last resort, "Our senses are deceiving us. There is no gardener, no blooms, no palace, and no officials. It's all a hoax!"

Finally the believing explorer despaired, "But what remains of your original assertion? Just how does this mirage differ from a real gardener?"

By John Frame

(*Jesus Among Other Gods*, pp.166–67)

Summarize what you think the author of the first parable is trying to say.
There is no difference between a God who won't come down and prove His existence to us and a God who doesn't exist at all. It's a "seeing is believing" approach: since I can't see Him, He doesn't exist.

Leader Notes

Have you encountered people with this view, and if so, what stands out in your memory regarding any conversations about God you have had with them?
These people generally don't want to believe—this is often the first of a series of arguments they may put forth to defend their disbelief.

Summarize what you think the author of the second parable is trying to say.
There is a God and He has done everything possible to prove His existence to us. Those who don't see Him are stubbornly refusing to listen.

How does this second parable undermine the point made by the nonbelievers in the first parable?
Some people say that they won't believe in God until they have adequate proof of His existence. But once they have been given enough tangible proof they then insist it is a hoax, or try to explain it with a different conclusion. Ultimately, neither proof nor lack of proof will ever convince them. God will have to work in their life.

Read or have a group member read the following summary of Ravi's garden themes.

Ravi breaks down the uniqueness of Christianity into four main themes, each of which is represented by a different "garden":

First garden—referred to by Ravi as the "text" of life. The setting for this is the Garden of Eden. It is where God created us and outlined how we should live. He provided us with the ground rules for life.

Second garden—referred to by Ravi as the "context" for living. The setting for this is the desert where Jesus was tempted. It represents the temptations we have all faced since Adam and Eve—did God really mean what He said? Can we reinterpret God's words for our own purposes?

Third garden—what Ravi calls the "contest" for our souls. The setting for this is the Garden of Gethsemane. It is where Jesus was betrayed and arrested, which led to His crucifixion. It was the moment where Jesus committed to following God's will as He started down the path to the death that would set us free.

Fourth garden—where Ravi positions the "conquest" of death. The setting here is the garden outside Jesus' tomb. It is where Mary witnesses the resurrected Christ. It is the culminating moment of Jesus' ministry and the most unique aspect of Christianity compared to other religions.

Refer to the above outline and your notes as you study each "garden."

The First Garden
Ravi says in the video that too often, "we get bogged down in the wrong question . . . did He create [the world] in six days or is this universe fifteen billion years old?" He then outlines four major "realities" we can draw from the book of Genesis that go beyond this argument about evolution vs. creationism:

1. God is the creator and He is both personal and eternal. He is a living, communicating God.

2. The world did not come by accident, but was designed with humanity in mind—man is an intelligent, spiritual being.

3. Life could not be lived out alone but through companionship—man is a relational, dependent being.

4. Man was fashioned as a moral entity with the privilege of self-determination—man is an accountable, rational being.

Focus your group discussion on the last two questions of this section.

Think about the description of creation in Genesis 1 (Open your Bible if you need your memory refreshed). What stands out to you as the most important aspect of this description?

_____

_____

_____

In this light, what does Genesis mean to you? How would you summarize the main points? (You don't have to reread the whole book to answer this question, but feel free to skim it over as a quick reminder of the major events.)

God gave us purpose and meaning. He gave us reasons for, explanations about, and examples of the meaning of life. He answers the "who, what, where, when, and why" questions of our existence.

_____

_____

_____

Ravi explains in his book, "You see, the real issue was not the explicability of the material world. The real issue was whether God had spoken through language as well as through nature.... Is there only a garden to look at, or is there also a voice with which the gardener speaks?" (p. 171). In what ways do you see people today denying that there is a "voice with which the gardener speaks"?

Existentialism, Nietzsche, and those who say "God is dead." Those who feel that God doesn't speak to us any more like He did in the Old Testament. To deny the truth of the Bible is to deny that God spoke....

_____

_____

_____

How could you use the text of Genesis to help someone who may be struggling to find a sense of purpose or meaning in this world?

God created us. He made each one of us. We're not a random conglomeration of atoms floating around in space. He's given us instructions for life, and He wants to have a personal relationship with us.

_____

_____

_____

Leader Notes

Direct people to focus on everything God is doing. God spoke. God gave purpose and meaning. It's all about what God has done, not a description meant to initiate controversy about the number of days, etc.

This question sets up comparisons to other religions and philosophical outlooks, so try to lead the discussion in that direction. Ravi addresses this when talking about the "context" for our lives and decisions—we have a moral framework in which we live.

Focus your group discussion on the second and third questions in this section.

The Second Garden

How can Christians discern what is right and what is wrong?

The Bible gives clear statements about what is right and wrong. The Holy Sprit guides and prompts us.

What are some of the subtle ways that you see people manipulating God's Word for their own needs?

Taking verses or parts of verses out of context to support their lifestyle. Abuses of this sort are rampant.

How have you been reinterpreting God's words for your own purposes? What specific actions can you take this week to turn back toward God?

Direct people to see that our focus should be, "What can I do for God?" and "How can I be obedient to God's Word?" not, "What can God do for me?" or "How can I use God's Word to back me up?"

The Third Garden

Many people today wear necklaces with crosses on them. Why does Christianity focus so much on the crucifixion? Why would someone wear a cross today? Do you think that most people understand the deep significance of this sign they wear?

The crucifixion is the focus because the death and resurrection of Jesus is at the heart of the gospel. Wearing a cross should remind us of His death for our sins and focus our thoughts on Jesus throughout the day. It is sad when it becomes merely a piece of jewelry.

Describe briefly what the cross has meant to you in your life.

_____

_____

_____

In the video Ravi quotes a theologian named Martin Hengel as saying, "Reflection on the harsh reality of crucifixion in antiquity may help us overcome the acute loss of reality which is to be found so often in present theology and teaching." Quite often we encounter people who say that Christianity is a "crutch," something we use to avoid the harsh realities of life. How does an examination of what happened on the cross invalidate such a challenge?

_____

_____

_____

The cross represents, among other things, obedience to God, something He calls us to throughout the Bible, and in all aspects of our lives. In the Garden of Gethsemane Jesus realized fully the pain that lay ahead of Him, and He had the option to flee or avoid the suffering. That would have been the easy thing to do. However, He chose the path of obedience to God, a path that would lead to suffering, humiliation, torture, and death. And a death that was completely undeserved, a death that wasn't just for the well-behaved people or the do-gooders of this world, but for the most abject sinful people who don't "deserve" anything in our eyes. He died for us all, out of willing obedience to His father's will.

The Christian walk is by no means an easy option. Accepting Christ doesn't guarantee us wealth or happiness. The Bible isn't another self-help book. It is the truth, plain and simple, and God demands us to be obedient to His Word. We fail all the time, but we are covered by the death of Jesus and called to keep striving toward the goal. Jesus Himself notes many times throughout His ministry that to follow Him will result in suffering and persecution. Look at the underground church in China, or the plight of Christians in Sudan. Even in American society there is increasing discrimination against those who hold the Bible to be true. In schools, children are made out to be stupid; in colleges, Christians are mocked as being intellectually deficient. In politics Christians are ridiculed and lambasted for being too conservative, too uppity, too moral. And all the time the world is beckoning you to succumb to sin and pursue earthly pleasures instead.

Spiritually, the battle is fierce as well. Satan doesn't need to waste much time or energy on nonbelievers, but he spends a lot of time and energy trying to lead believers away from the fold. To model our lives on Jesus is to submit to a life of self-sacrifice and self-control, of committing our lives and desires to His will on a daily basis. It is a life of obedience, hardly something that can be dismissed as a "crutch" for weak people.

The Fourth Garden

What reaction have you had to the resurrection of Jesus and the power of life over death that it represents?

Ravi mentions in the video the many Hindus in India who go to great lengths to seek atonement and peace in their lives, without recognizing that Jesus has already paid the price for them. (He talks about self-mutilation with spears and daggers, rites of fire and pain, washing in "sacred" waters, making pilgrimages, etc.) How do you think people here in the Western world do similar things in an effort to achieve "atonement" and peace?
Just look at the number of books in the self-help section of your bookstore. Also, people indulge in drugs, sexual immorality, obsessive eating or dieting, obsessive workouts, desire for money, etc. . . .

Bible Focus
Read John 1:1–14.

In the beginning was the Word, and the Word was with God, and the Word was God. He was in the beginning with God. All things were made through Him, and without Him nothing was made that was made. In Him was life, and the life was the light of men. And the light shines in the darkness, and the darkness did not comprehend it.
There was a man sent from God, whose name was John. This man came for a witness, to bear witness of the Light, that all through him might believe. He was not that Light, but was sent to bear witness of that Light. That was the true Light which gives light to every man coming into the world.
He was in the world, and the world was made through Him, and the world did not know Him. He came to His own, and His own did not receive Him. But as many as received Him, to them He gave the right to become children of God, even to those who believe in His name: who were born, not of blood, nor of the will of the flesh, nor of the will of man, but of God. And the Word became flesh and dwelt among us, and we beheld His glory, the glory as of the only begotten of the Father, full of grace and truth.

Have someone keep Genesis 1 open because some questions will refer to that passage. If the small groups worked well in the last session, use the same approach here, assigning each of the first three passages to a small group for study and report, then tackling the final passage with the entire group.
20 Minutes

Who is "the Word"?
Words are the essence of communication. Jesus, as "the Word" is the sole link between us and God.

Leader Notes

Who was present at the creation?
God the Father, Jesus, and the Holy Spirit.

"And the light shines in the darkness, and the darkness did not comprehend it.... He was in the world, and the world was made through Him, and the world did not know Him." **Why do you think it is so hard for people to recognize and understand Jesus?**
We are too proud (like the Pharisees), we are stubborn (like Pilate), and we have wrong expectations (like Herod and the rich young ruler).

Read Luke 4:1–13.
Then Jesus, being filled with the Holy Spirit, returned from the Jordan and was led by the Spirit into the wilderness, being tempted for forty days by the devil. And in those days He ate nothing, and afterward, when they had ended, He was hungry. And the devil said to Him, "If You are the Son of God, command this stone to become bread."
But Jesus answered him, saying, "It is written, 'Man shall not live by bread alone, but by every word of God.' "
Then the devil, taking Him up on a high mountain, showed Him all the kingdoms of the world in a moment of time. And the devil said to Him, "All this authority I will give You, and their glory; for this has been delivered to me, and I give it to whomever I wish. Therefore, if You will worship before me, all will be Yours."
And Jesus answered and said to him, "Get behind Me, Satan! For it is written, 'You shall worship the LORD your God, and Him only you shall serve.' "
Then he brought Him to Jerusalem, set Him on the pinnacle of the temple, and said to Him, "If You are the Son of God, throw Yourself down from here. For it is written:
'He shall give His angels charge over you,
To keep you,'
"and,
'In their hands they shall bear you up,
Lest you dash your foot against a stone.' "
And Jesus answered and said to him, "It has been said, 'You shall not tempt the LORD your God.' "
Now when the devil had ended every temptation, he departed from Him until an opportune time.

Jesus was alone in the desert for 40 days. Think about this—for almost a month and a half He was alone, without food, and being tempted. In contrast our temptations are minor and short-lived. List some of the emotions and thoughts He must have experienced.

Loneliness, sadness, abandonment, helplessness, hunger, possessing the power to change the world but wanting to do God's will, frustration, and anger at Satan.

Summarize in your own words the three temptations and how Jesus responded to them.

The temptations are pretty obvious, but you can focus on the root of them all—Satan was tempting Jesus to disobedience and pride, to taking the easy way out.

Whom or what did Jesus turn to in His time of struggle? How did He know what to say?

The Scriptures. This should encourage us to memorize Scripture so we have something to turn to in times of need.

When we encounter temptations, to whom or what do we tend to turn?

Sometimes we turn to the wrong place—other people. Our first step should be to look to God for help and guidance. Later we can seek the counsel of others, or God may help us and answer prayer by providing people who can help. But the first step should always be to prayer.

When you are making decisions, how do you know you are making the right ones?
Through prayer, searching the Scripture for similar situations, and the counsel of mature Christians.

Leader Notes

Read John 19:1–18.
So then Pilate took Jesus and scourged Him. And the soldiers twisted a crown of thorns and put it on His head, and they put on Him a purple robe. Then they said, "Hail, King of the Jews!" And they struck Him with their hands.

Pilate then went out again, and said to them, "Behold, I am bringing Him out to you, that you may know that I find no fault in Him." Then Jesus came out, wearing the crown of thorns and the purple robe. And Pilate said to them, "Behold the Man!"

Therefore, when the chief priests and officers saw Him, they cried out, saying, "Crucify Him, crucify Him!"

Pilate said to them, "You take Him and crucify Him, for I find no fault in Him."

The Jews answered him, "We have a law, and according to our law He ought to die, because He made Himself the Son of God."

Therefore, when Pilate heard that saying, he was the more afraid, and went again into the Praetorium, and said to Jesus, "Where are You from?" But Jesus gave him no answer.

Then Pilate said to Him, "Are You not speaking to me? Do You not know that I have power to crucify You, and power to release You?"

Jesus answered, "You could have no power at all against Me unless it had been given you from above. Therefore the one who delivered Me to you has the greater sin."

From then on Pilate sought to release Him, but the Jews cried out, saying, "If you let this Man go, you are not Caesar's friend. Whoever makes himself a king speaks against Caesar."

When Pilate therefore heard that saying, he brought Jesus out and sat down in the judgment seat in a place that is called The Pavement, but in Hebrew, Gabbatha. Now it was the Preparation Day of the Passover, and about the sixth hour. And he said to the Jews, "Behold your King!"

But they cried out, "Away with Him, away with Him! Crucify Him!"

Pilate said to them, "Shall I crucify your King?"

The chief priests answered, "We have no king but Caesar!"

Then he delivered Him to them to be crucified. So they took Jesus and led Him away.

And He, bearing His cross, went out to a place called the Place of a Skull, which is called in Hebrew, Golgotha, where they crucified Him, and two others with Him, one on either side, and Jesus in the center.

What aspect of Jesus' humiliation do you find most clearly indicates the lack of respect demonstrated by those who put Jesus to death?

_____

_____

How did Jesus still exhibit godliness during His trial and crucifixion despite His surroundings?
He didn't struggle or try to flee. He didn't try to appease or argue with those who accused Him. He knew what was coming, and His attitude reflected His obedience to God's will. Just look at how He responded to Caiaphas, Herod, and Pilate.

_____

_____

_____

Why do you think Jesus didn't answer Pilate's question, "Where do you come from?"
The text says that as soon as Pilate heard that Jesus claimed to be the Son of God, he was afraid. Jesus knew that Pilate knew the answer to his question before he asked it. Jesus didn't need to say anything further. Indeed, Pilate proclaimed Jesus as the king of the Jews and tried to free Him.

_____

_____

_____

Read John 19:41–20:16.
Now in the place where He was crucified there was a garden, and in the garden a new tomb in which no one had yet been laid. So there they laid Jesus, because of the Jews' Preparation Day, for the tomb was nearby.
Now on the first day of the week Mary Magdalene went to the tomb early, while it was still dark, and saw that the stone had been taken away from the tomb. Then she ran and came to Simon Peter, and to the other disciple, whom Jesus loved, and said to them, "They have taken away the Lord out of the tomb, and we do not know where they have laid Him."
Peter therefore went out, and the other disciple, and were going to the tomb. So they both ran together, and the other disciple outran Peter and came to the tomb first. And he, stooping down and looking in, saw the linen cloths lying there; yet he did not go in. Then Simon Peter came, following him, and went into the tomb; and he saw the linen cloths lying there, and the handkerchief that had been around His head, not lying with the linen cloths, but folded together in a place by itself. Then the other disciple, who came to the tomb first, went in also; and he saw and believed. For as yet they did not know the Scripture, that He must rise again from the dead. Then the disciples went away again to their own homes.

But Mary stood outside by the tomb weeping, and as she wept she stooped down and looked into the tomb. And she saw two angels in white sitting, one at the head and the other at the feet, where the body of Jesus had lain. Then they said to her, "Woman, why are you weeping?" She said to them, "Because they have taken away my Lord, and I do not know where they have laid Him." Now when she had said this, she turned around and saw Jesus standing there, and did not know that it was Jesus. Jesus said to her, "Woman, why are you weeping? Whom are you seeking?" She, supposing Him to be the gardener, said to Him, "Sir, if You have carried Him away, tell me where You have laid Him, and I will take Him away." Jesus said to her, "Mary!" She turned and said to Him, "Rabboni!" (which is to say, Teacher).

What details of this account strike you as particularly significant in demonstrating the truthfulness of the witnesses?

_____

_____

_____

Even when they saw the empty tomb, the disciples still did not understand that He had risen from the dead. In what ways is this reaction a common human reaction?
We tend to need a context or precedent for us to be able to believe something. We don't think of the possibility of resurrection until after it's happened. It's an event that is mind-boggling and defies all the laws of biology and medicine that we know of.

_____

_____

_____

When Jesus said, "Mary," what thought processes do you think triggered her recognition of Him?
Jesus called Mary by her name. It was an intimate, personal connection that reflects Jesus' desire to know and have a relationship with each one of us as individuals. She must have heard such overwhelming love, compassion, understanding, and tenderness in His voice.

_____

_____

Leader Notes

Particularly if this session runs long, you may want to schedule a further sharing time when the group can gather and reflect on the entire study. If the process has had, in Ravi's own words, a life-trans-forming effect, the group would be a wonderful place to begin expressing that change to others.
Up to 10 Minutes

Taking It Home
Reread the final paragraph of Jesus' exchange with Mary in the last section.

How is Jesus "more than a gardener"?
He sacrificed Himself for our sins. Look back at the answers to the first warm-up question. God does more than merely tend His creation; through Jesus He sanctified us, making us whole once again. In the garden of God's creation we are all inflicted with the same fatal disease, and there is no natural-ly available cure. But God, out of love for us, has healed us with the blood of Jesus. That is the heart of the gospel message—Jesus' power to conquer death once and for all.

_____

_____

_____

Ravi talks about the "reality of forgive-ness." God knows exactly who you are. Take some time to write down all the ways in which God has forgiven you.

_____

_____

_____

How is Jesus similar to Mohammed, Buddha, and some parts of Hinduism?
They all talked about the meaning of life and pro-vided different ways to overcome or deal with the struggles of life. They have all impacted large num-bers of people.

_____

_____

_____

How is Jesus different?
He is the only one who rose from the dead and who seeks a personal relationship with each of us. He is the only one to claim to be God and to fulfill numerous prophecies regarding His life and divinity.

_____

_____

At the tomb, Mary didn't recognize Jesus

until He said her name—He made a personal connection with her. In our faith, we know from the Bible that the Lord chooses us—He calls us each by name. **How is this different from Buddhism/Hinduism?**

God loves and cares and died for each one of us. Buddhism and Hinduism focus on becoming part of the "whole." A goal is to lose your sense of self, your sense of identity; to do away with what makes you unique and special in God's eyes. In Buddhism the self is lost. In Hinduism the self is divinized. But God calls out to each one of us as individuals. He invites us to a relationship with Him.

_____

_____

_____

How is this approach different from the philosophies of nonbelievers who are seeking a "religion"?

They are looking for a "religion," an "outlook" on life, something they can tailor to suit their own lives which will require the least amount of work or change as possible. Many people pick and choose what they want to believe; it is incomprehensible to them that God would want them specifically, and they are not ready to accept one absolute truth.

_____

_____

_____

To what degree are you convinced of the unique nature of Jesus Christ? How has this study deepened your faith or your understanding of Jesus?

_____

_____

_____

Leader Notes

Remind the group that the Scriptures are filled with illustrations of the truths they have been studying. Encourage them to read the parables of the prodigal son, or the lost coin, or the lost sheep, or read the prophet Hosea, or the other prophets. Despite Israel's sin God still sought them out and wanted to rekindle the relationship. God is not an "absent landlord." He is very much present and alive and He wants a relationship with you.

Close the study with prayer, asking God to help the group retain the lessons learned and to recall them when speaking to others about Jesus.

About Ravi Zacharias

Although you will have gleaned a good deal of autobiographical insight about Ravi from the video presentation, a few additional words about this representative of Jesus Christ might be helpful.

Ravi Zacharias is president of Ravi Zacharias International Ministries. Born in India, he has lectured in more than fifty countries and in several of the world's most prominent universities. For more information on these ministries, visit their web site www.rzim.org.

He is author of numerous books, including *Can Man Live without God, Deliver Us from Evil,* and *Cries of the Heart.*

Ravi's weekly radio program, "Let My People Think," is heard on numerous radio stations across the country.

Ravi and his wife, Margie, are the parents of three children.